The
Quatrefoil of Love

EARLY ENGLISH TEXT SOCIETY

Original Series, No. 195

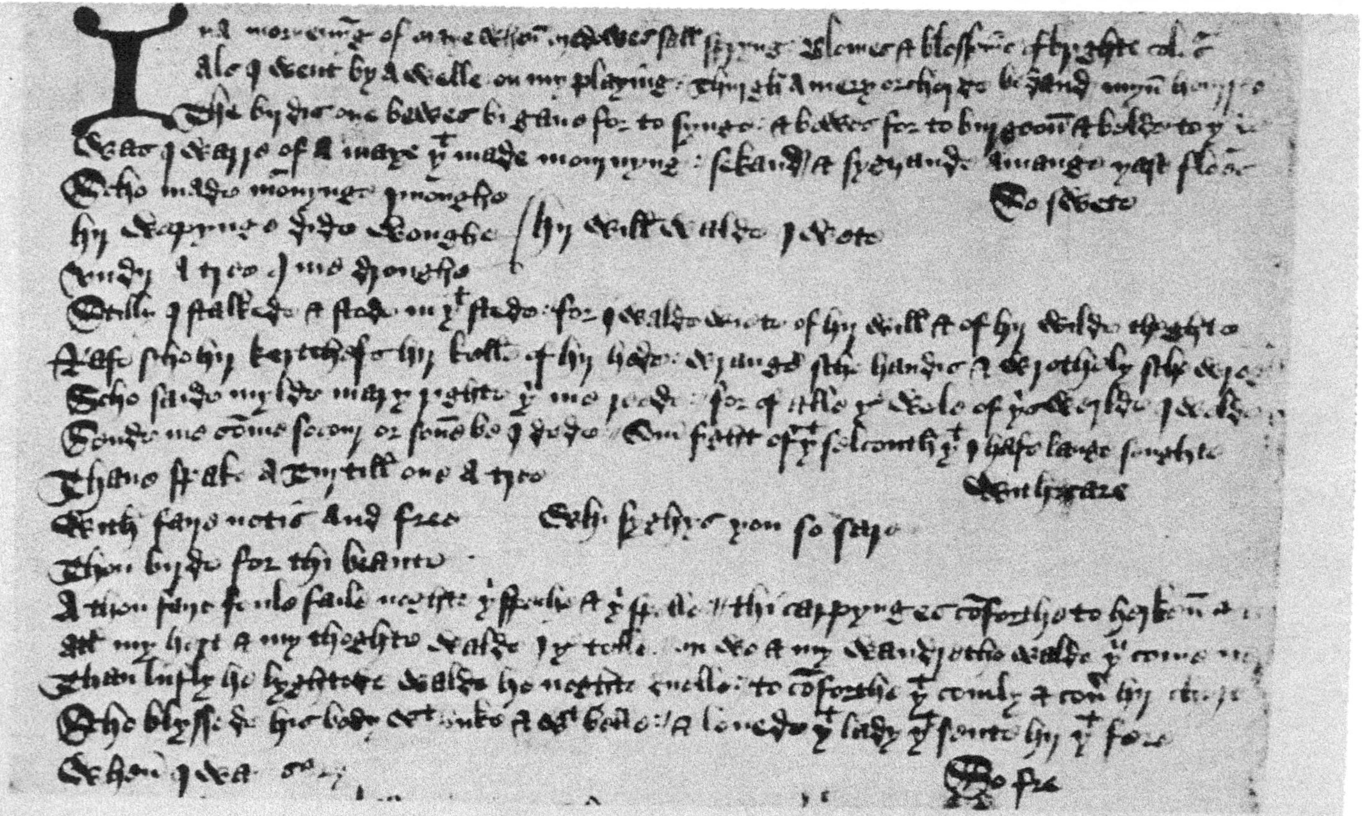

British Museum MS. Additional 31042, fol. 98 a

The Quatrefoil of Love

EDITED FROM
BRIT. MUS. MS. ADD. 31042 WITH
COLLATIONS FROM BODL. MS. ADD. A 106

BY

Sir ISRAEL GOLLANCZ, Litt.D., F.B.A.

AND

MAGDALENE M. WEALE, M.A.

LONDON:
PUBLISHED FOR THE EARLY ENGLISH TEXT SOCIETY
BY HUMPHREY MILFORD, OXFORD UNIVERSITY PRESS
AMEN HOUSE, E.C. 4

OXFORD
UNIVERSITY PRESS

Great Clarendon Street, Oxford OX2 6DP
United Kingdom

Oxford University Press is a department of the University of Oxford.
It furthers the University's objective of excellence in research, scholarship,
and education by publishing worldwide. Oxford is a registered trade mark of
Oxford University Press in the UK and in certain other countries

© The Early English Text Society 1935

The moral rights of the authors have been asserted

Database right Oxford University Press (maker)

First Edition published in 1935

All rights reserved. No part of this publication may be reproduced,
stored in a retrieval system, or transmitted, in any form or by any means,
without the prior permission in writing of Oxford University Press,
or as expressly permitted by law, or under terms agreed with the appropriate
reprographics rights organization. Enquiries concerning reproduction
outside the scope of the above should be sent to the Rights Department,
Oxford University Press, at the address above

You must not circulate this book in any other form
and you must impose this same condition on any acquirer

Published in the United States of America by Oxford University Press
198 Madison Avenue, New York, NY 10016, United States of America

British Library Cataloguing in Publication Data
Data available

Library of Congress Cataloging in Publication Data
Data available

Original Series, 195

ISBN 978-0-85-991929-6

PREFATORY NOTE

SIR ISRAEL GOLLANCZ had intended to issue *The Quatrefoil of Love* in his series of *Select Early English Poems*, and at the time of his death both the text and collations had been set up in type. These have now been checked with the manuscripts by Miss Magdalene M. Weale, who completed for the Society *The Book of the Foundation of St. Bartholomew's Church in London*, left unfinished by the late Sir Norman Moore. The Society is also indebted to Miss Weale for supplying the Introduction, Notes, and Glossary to the present volume.

A. W. P.

8 *August* 1934

INTRODUCTION

The Manuscripts. There are two known manuscripts of *The Quatrefoil of Love*: Additional MS. British Museum 31042, which we call A, and Additional MS. Bodleian A 106, referred to as B. Additional MS. 31042, which is the basis of our text, was acquired by the British Museum in 1879. It is a quarto volume of the fifteenth century, in a modern binding of dark blue half-morocco with corners and gold lines, and it contains one of the famous collections of English poems and romances made by Robert Thornton, of East Newton, Yorkshire, the compiler of a similar collection in folio preserved in the Lincoln Cathedral Library.

The British Museum volume contains 179 paper folios, measuring 27·4 × 20·2 centimetres, with four additional pages of vellum, two at the beginning and two at the end, which were part of the original binding of the book. There is no original pagination, and these vellum folios, which are fly-leaves from a fifteenth-century Breviary, are now numbered 1, 2, 182, and 183 respectively. Apart from some few lines of Latin doggerel on f. 97 v., and some Latin titles, colophons, notes, and quotations, the book is in English and contains twenty-six items, among which are the interesting *Parlement of the Thre Ages* and *Wynnere and Wastoure*. Two of the poems have the name of the compiler written at the end, both in the same bold script. On f. 50, at the end of the *Passion of Our Lord*, the signature: *R. Thornton*, has been partly erased and disfigured, and on f. 66, after *The Segge of Jerusalem*, appears the following legend: *R. Thornton dictus qui scripsit sit benedictus Amen*, with the surname written over and changed to another name which is indecipherable.

The script of the volume is a book-hand of the fifteenth century, written partly in double columns. The manuscript is in a fairly good state of preservation, though two pages have been torn out after f. 110, ff. 145 and 152 have been badly mutilated, and the edges of other pages have been torn, cut, or worn away. The ink in parts is of a faded brown colour.

The large initial letters are mostly rubricated, though blue is used on f. 9 v. and green on f. 120, and green alternates with red on ff. 104–119 v., and again, though less regularly, on ff. 144 v.–161 v. On f. 163 v. *The Romance of the Childhode of Jhesu Criste* begins with an

A, part green and part blue, and green initials appear again on ff. 166 and 166 v. There are rough black ink drawings on ff. 33 and 50. The book, unlike the Lincoln volume (see Halliwell: *The Thornton Romances*, pp. xxv-vi), affords no evidence that it remained for any length of time in the Thornton family; a century or so later we find it is in the possession of one John Nettleton, for at the top of f. 49 is written, in a hand not earlier than the mid-sixteenth century: *John Nettletons Boke*, and on f. 139 v. his surname is inscribed again four times, in each case in a post early-sixteenth century hand.

The Quatrefoil of Love is the twelfth item in the volume and occupies ff. 98–101 v. It follows some verses in Latin and English, and is itself followed by a hymn to the Holy Ghost, written immediately below it on f. 101 v. There is no signature or colophon, neither is there a heading, the title given to the poem in this edition being the suggestion of the late Sir Israel Gollancz. The poem is written two verses to the line for the first eight verses or metrical lines, the metrical division between each pair being denoted by a colon and slanting bar, which is sometimes single, sometimes double. The ninth short verse or metrical line is written well out to the right of the page, on a line with the tenth verse which is bracketed, on the left side of the page, with the eleventh and twelfth verses which rime with it. The final verse of the stanza appears on the right of the bracket, close up to it, and occupies the middle of the page. The poem so written falls naturally into its stanzaic formation which is not otherwise denoted, and there are, roughly, five stanzas to the page.

The first initial alone is rubricated; there are no catchwords and no systematic punctuation.[1] The handwriting differs in size in places, but the poem is written throughout by the same scribe. Folio 98 has been torn and repaired, and the edges of all the pages are damaged, so that several words of the text, especially at the ends of lines, are illegible or missing. The ink is brown.

The poem is written in a clear hand and the abbreviations are not numerous. Of the ordinary contractions we find $þ^t$, $þ^u$, w^t, for *þat*, *þou*, *with*, and the usual signs for *ur* and *ra*. Less usually, the scribe writes t^eson for *treson* in l. 133, whereas superscribed *a* does not denote the omission of *r* in the name *Thomas* (ll. 288, 290, and 291).

[1] Colons and full stops appear occasionally in the text, doing the work of commas, e.g. after *welle* in l. 3 and after *saulde* in l. 174, and in l. 157 each word is followed by a colon.

Introduction ix

The turn-up sign is used for *er* except after *p*, where *p̄* is employed, and in ll. 240 and 314 we find *ħt* for *hert*. The scribe makes no distinction between I and J, and *Jhu* is the usual contraction for *Jhesu*. Final *d* sometimes has a tail; only when this tail is very definite and the spelling with *e* conforms to the usual practice of the scribe, have I extended tailed *d* to *de*; *w̄* is printed *w̄*, but the turn-up in *w̄* and *m̄*, having evidently no significance, has been disregarded and *n* and *m* appear in the printed text. The contraction *&* has been extended to *and*; *tt̄*, *g*, and *t* are printed as they appear in the manuscript, though the crossings seem to mean nothing; *þⁱ* and *þᵉ* are kept unaltered, but *þⁱs* is printed as *þis*. The symbols *y* and *þ* are confused throughout the manuscript, and these I have altered where necessary. Capital letters have been kept as the scribe wrote them, except that each printed metrical line begins with a capital whether it is in the manuscript or not.

The contraction for the nasal is the only one that presents any difficulty, ⌒- ⌒ ⌒- — being used indiscriminately. The sign ⌒, however, seems to stand for *e* in *Egippe* in l. 164, and on the strength of this I have extended *blossom̄s* to *blossomes* in l. 2 [1] and *baroūns* to *barounes* in l. 446. In *wȳnnes* in l. 346 the contraction sign is evidently a mistake. There is, of course, no distinction between *u* and *n* in the manuscript.

Deletions from the text of MS. A are denoted by an arrow, and additions of words or parts of words not in MS. A, including those missing at the ends of lines where the edges of the MS. are damaged, are enclosed in square brackets.

The Bodleian MS. A 106, which we call B, gives us a less good version of the poem, but it has been of great value in the restoration of the text. The book containing *The Quatrefoil of Love* consists of six manuscripts written in the fifteenth century in the north of England, and bound together in a contemporary binding of ruled brown leather on boards, with a leather thong. Some pages are disfigured, but otherwise the MS. is in good condition. Except for five thirteenth-century vellum fly-leaves, three at the beginning and two at the end, which are in Latin, the book is written in English, on 282 leaves of paper measuring 20·5 × 14·5 cms. The pagination is modern. On f. 196 v. is written: *Thys ys Jhn̄s pryste Booke*, on f. 197 v.: *Jhn Innan̄*

---

[1] The final *s* looks like *e* subsequently changed, as if the scribe had intended writing *blossommes*.

and *Jhon pr̄*, and on f. 277 v. : *harry foustoñ*. These may represent early owners of the book or part of it.

The Quatrefoil of Love is the second item in the book and occupies ff. 6 v.–14 v. ; it follows the first item, a medical treatise, on the same page on which that leaves off, and is itself followed by a lullaby on f. 14 v. There is no title, colophon, or signature. It is written one verse to a line ; the riming lines are bracketed together in red, except for ll. 9 and 13 of each stanza, which rime together and are written out to the right of the page. The stanzas are denoted by a red paragraph sign at the beginning of each, and there are, roughly, just over two stanzas to a page. A large red initial begins the poem, and the initial of every metrical line or verse is rubricated. It is written throughout by the same scribe, the latter part in a brownish, slightly faded ink. There is no punctuation. The contractions are rather more numerous than in A. Among these, besides the usual abbreviations for *ur, ra, er,* and *es*, we find p^t for *þat*, p^u for *þou*, w^t for *with*, crossed *p* for *per* and *par*, crossed long *s* for *ser*, tailed *d* for *de*, ꝑ for *re*, superscribed *i* for *ri*, and for the nasal abbreviation, — and ⁀ ; we also find the turn-up after the nasal and after *g*. As in A, the symbols *y* and *þ* are confused.

Printed Editions. The text of the poem, under the title : *The Quatrefoil of Love*, with a prefatory note, was first published by Sir Israel Gollancz in *An English Miscellany. Presented to Dr. Furnivall*, etc. (1901). It was printed from the text of MS. A after collation with MS. B, some variant readings from which are given. There are no notes or glossary. It was the intention of the editor to produce an annotated edition, and the text for this proposed publication was set up in 1912. Only the text, with variant readings, was prepared, and this I have completely revised and collated with both manuscripts for this edition. Those emendations of the text which have been retained from the 1912 proof I have distinguished in the Notes.

Orthography of the Manuscript. In manuscript A of the poem *y* always denotes *i*.

u in the vicinity of letters resembling it in shape is, according to the usual practice, written *o* in such words as *soñ* and *wone*; and we ave *u* for *w*, and *w* for *u*.

Except initially (where we find *v*) *u* and *v* are interchangeable, as are *i* and *j*.

ē is sometimes written *e*, at other times *ee*.

Introduction

OE. *ĭg* which has become final appears as *ey*, *ye* (both with the sound of *ī*, to judge by the rimes), e.g. *ey*, *hye*. We find, however, the Northern consonantal spelling *egh* in *eghne* (compare singular *ey*), and *heghe* beside *hey*, *hye*.

ōh, *ōg*, is written *ough* in *ynoughe*, *woughe*, *droughe* in MS. A but *ogh* in B ; *ōh(t)* in A and B is written *og(t)*, *ogh(t)*, and also, in MS. A, *ough(t)*.

ȝ is used for consonantal *y*.

th and *þ* are interchangeable ; *y* and *þ* are confused in both MSS. In MS. A the parasitic glide between *a* and a following *l* is written *u* in *haulle* (riming with *salle*) and *saulde*, 'sold'.

Language. The provenance of both manuscripts of our poem is the north of England, and it appears certain that the original work was composed in the Northern dialect.

I. The forms are Northern, with some admixture of Midland forms :

(i) Words in which OE. *ā* remains abound. This sound rimes with OE. *a* in *care* : *sare* (ii) ; *tane* : *gane* (xii), and with OF. *a* in *gane* : *pane* (xxxi). Other examples of the survival are :[1] *alane* (402), *bane*, *blawe*, *clathe*, *famen*, *gaste* (135), *halde*, *haly*, *hatte* (380), *knawe*, *lande*, *lare* (367), *mare* (193, 239, 376, 462, 507), *maste* (131), *nane*, *sary*, *swa*, *wa*, *wate* (384), *wha*.

But the rimes of *one* with *trone* (vii), of *folde* with *golde* (xii) are Midland, and in *fonne* : *sone* (xxviii) we have ON. *ā* riming with OE. *ō*. Other Midland forms in this text are: *also* (178), *bone*, *goo* (103), *holy*, *more*, *non*, *so*, *solde*, *wolde* (153), *wo(o)* (101, 182), *who*. We also find *bothe* and *froo* (102) corresponding to the forms with ON. *ā*.

The rimes *woo* : *froo* : *goo* (viii), *solde* : *wolde* : *bolde* : *tolde* (xv), where MS. B has the *a* rimes, and ot *also* : *wo* (xiv), where B has the Midland *o* forms, may be alterations by a Midland scribe, but not necessarily so. If he altered these rimes it seems strange that he should have left unchanged such rimes as those in stanza xvi, *allañ* : *bane* : *gane* : *nane*.

Therefore it appears that our author keeps Northern *ā* on the whole but has a few Midland forms.

(ii) OE. mutation *ǣ* > open *ē* in *dele* (472), but > close *ē* before a dental in *lere* (60, 172), and is shortened to *e* in *cledde* (433). OE. *ǣ*[1] > close *ē* in *strete* (42), *bere* (358), *drede* (386, 482, 499), *were* (410),

[1] Those words occurring in significant rimes have the line-references added in brackets after them.

dede (484, 501), *rede* (486); but it rimes with open *ē* in stanza ii, *stede* : *hede* : *reede* : *dede*. In stanza xv, *drede* : *lede*, we have OE. *ǣ*¹ and mutation *ǣ* riming together before a dental.

(iii) The rime of OE. *ā* with *ai* in *maste* : *trayste* (xi) looks like the Scotch and S. Yorks. *ai* becoming *ā* (see Jordan, *Handbuch der ME. Grammatik*, p. 123).

(iv) Our text shows consistently the Midland raising of OE. *ēg* to *ī*, e.g. *hey* : *trye* : *crye* : *dye* (xv) ; *hy* : *ey* (xxiii); *I* : *gentry* : *hye* : *wry* (xxxvii).

(v) OE *ȳ* (*ṻ*) becomes NE. Midland *ī*, e.g. *begyn̈*: *syn* (xxxvii) ; *fyre* : *syre* (xxxiii).

(vi) Northern *u* for OE. *ō* is seen in *buke*, *blude* (though *blode* is the usual form), and *gude* (*gode* never occurring). We have also *tuk* beside *toke*, 'took'.

(vii) We find Northern *k* for OE. *c* in the words: *blenke*, *swilk*, *wrenke*, and Northern and N. Midland *k* in *ilk*, *mekill*.

(viii) We have the Northern forms *sall*, *solde*, *sulde* side by side with the Midland forms in *sch-*, *schall*, *scholde*.

II. The accidence, too, is Northern. No plural noun in *-en* (except the Northern *eghne*) is to be found, *-es*, *-is* (*-ys*), and *-s*(*e*) being the usual terminations of plural nouns. The Northern and North Midland *childer*, *childre*, *childir*, occurs. Apart from the uninflected genitive singular of the strong masculine *fadir*, which occurs twice, and of the weak feminine *hert* (occurring twice) and *trewlufe*, the only genitive singular form found in the text is *goddis*, beside the uninflected form *God*.

The pronouns are, on the whole, Northern: *scho*, *þay*, *þam*, *þair*(*e*) occur beside *þer*, *theire*. We find the Northern demonstratives *þase*, 'those', and *thire*, *þer*, 'these', beside *thies*, *þis*. *Slyk*, *swilk*, *swylk* are typical Northern forms, the use of *slyk*, according to Morris (see his edition of *The Pricke of Conscience*, p. viii), betokening a Border dialect of English. MS. B, however, reads *swylk* not *slyk* in l. 188.

Our text uses *sen*, 'since', as the conjunction, reserving *sythen*, *sythyn* for the adverb of time. This distinction is, according to Morris, characteristic of the Northern dialect used south of the Tweed. This distinction, however, is not observed in MS. B, which reads *syne* in l. 90.

The fourteenth-century use of *bot* in the senses of ME. *bout*, including its use as a preposition meaning ' without ', is, according to

Introduction

O.E.D., characteristic of the Northern dialect and especially of Scotch; but the one instance in our text of its prepositional use: *bot triste* (l. 385), is a doubtful one for, in that phrase, *bot* may be the conjunction 'but' followed by the infinitive 'to trust'.

We have the superlatives *ratheste, beste* (stanza iv) riming with *feste*.

The use of *at* as a preposition meaning 'to', before an infinitive of purpose, of *till* as a preposition meaning 'to' (each occurring three times) and of *untill*, 'unto', *intill*, 'into', is characteristic of the Northern dialect.

The verbs, too, are Northern in their forms. The final -*n* of the preterite plural does not exist in our text, and that of the infinitive is very rare, *gane*, the three times it occurs (ll. 146, 171, 200), being required for the rime and therefore original.

The -*n* of the strong past participle is retained, e.g. *tane* : *nane* (xii); *gane* : *pane* (xxxi); *lorne* : *bi-forne* : *borne* : *morne* (ix). The present participle ends invariably in -*and*(*e*), the suffix -*ing*, *yng*(*e*) being reserved for the verbal noun, e.g. *spryng* : *playing* : *synge* : *mournyng* (i).

In *gan*(*e*), *bigane*, we have strong preterite plurals with the vowel of the singular, as is usual in the Northern dialect. Characteristic of that dialect also is the use, as in our text, of the same form for the singular and plural present of the preterite-present verbs, *sall*, *may* and *wete*. In stanza xi we have the plural *sall* riming with *alle* ; in stanza xxvi, plural *may* rimes with *pray* and *clay*, and in stanza xxx we find plural *wate* riming with *late*.

The inflexional endings of the present indicative are also Northern: -*is* (-*ys*) appears three times as the ending of the second singular and we also have *þou sees*; the third singular ends generally in -*es*, with -*is* (-*ys*, -*ysse*) as a good second. The termination of the third plural is -*es* or -*e*, e.g. (*leues*) *sprynges* (305) ; (*gedlynges*) *kythes* (471); (*gladenesse and gudnesse*) *comforthes* (86) ; (*men*) *dele* : *catele* (xxxvii) ; (*clerkes*) *rede* : *dede* (xxxviii); (*þay*) *say* : *pray* (xxxiv). We have also the third plural present *hase*, 'have'.

Among the auxiliaries we find the Northern form of the second singular, (*þou*) *sall*, and in st. ix the rime (*þou*) *salle* : *calle* : *haulle*.

Traces of the Northern uninflected imperative occur : besides the usual second singular (all the forms of which in our text end in -*e*, except *trow*), we have the first plural *aske*, and the second plural *halde*. The past participles, *fune*, 'found', and *tane*, 'taken' (riming with *gane*) are also peculiar to the Northern dialect.

xiv   *Introduction*

III. Our text contains such characteristically Northern words as: *at* (preposition before infinitive), *barne, brathely, bus, emelle* (263), *fonne* (360), *gare, gate,* ' way ' (378), *sere* (406), *slyk, sterne, till,* ' to ', *tytte, wandrethe.*

The Quatrefoil of Love was, it is evident, originally composed in the Northern dialect of English. Though the text, as we know it, shows traces of alterations by a Midland scribe, this does not explain all the Midland forms. It seems likely that the original was composed in a district of the North close to the North Midland boundary, probably the NE. Midland boundary, judging by the change of OE. ў to *ī*. (See above under **Language**, I. v.)

Metre. Our poem belongs to the great revival of alliterative poetry which took place in the fourteenth century in the West Midlands and the North. In the West Midlands, where the revival originated, it continued in striking evidence for over a century, and in the North, where it reached the height of its popularity in the mid-fifteenth century, it survived until the sixteenth century.

The new alliterative line was based on the Old English alliterative line which normally had two strong accents in the first half-line alliterating with one in the second. Those fourteenth-century poems in which alliteration was unmixed with rime adhered more closely to the old line, but in the Northern group of romances and religious poems we note a tendency to excessive alliteration, and the line with four alliterating accents is the norm.

The combination of alliteration and rime is found in all types of medieval metre from the couplet to the elaborate stanzaic form of *Pearl.* In our poem we have the combination of the alliterative line with a Romance stanza consisting of two parts : (1) eight lines with four strong stresses and riming *abababab,* and (2) a ' wheel ' of five lines with two accents and riming *cdddc.* This alliterative stanza was especially popular in the North, where we find it as the metre of five poems of some length, apart from *The Quatrefoil of Love.* These are: *Golagros and Gawane, The Buke of the Howlat, Rauf Coilȝear, The Awntyrs off Arthure,* and *The Pistill of Susan,* all of which have been edited by F. J. Amours in *Scottish Alliterative Poems,* 1897. In all of these poems, except *The Pistill of Susan* and *The Quatrefoil of Love,* the first line of the 'wheel' has also four strong stresses; in the two exceptions it consists of a ' bob ' of two syllables with the accent on the last. Our poem is therefore linked by its stanzaic form to *The*

Introduction

Pistill of Susan which has, on the strength of a passage in Wyntoun's *Original Chronicle* (V. 4331-4334, been attributed to Huchoun 'of the Awle Ryale',

'That cunnand wes in litterature.
He maid þe gret Gest of Arthure,
And þe Anteris of Gawane,
The Epistill als of Suete Susane.'

On account of Dunbar's reference in his *Lament for the Makaris* (see ll. 53-68), Huchoun has been identified by some with Sir Hugh of Eglinton who flourished between 1348 and 1375.

The stanzaic form is the same, but the use of alliteration in the two poems is noticeably different. When all due allowance has been made for the vicissitudes which the text of *The Pistill of Susan* has experienced, the figures given below are indicative. F. J. Amours, on p. lxxxiii of *Scottish Alliterative Poems*, gives percentages of the various types of alliterative long lines in *The Pistill of Susan*. Dr. Oakden, on pp. 229-31 of *Alliterative Poetry in Middle English*, adopts Amours' figures and adds his own statistics for *The Quatrefoil of Love*. An examination of these two sets of figures reveals striking differences in the use of alliteration in the two poems. The figures for those types of lines which show most marked differences are quoted below. I have changed Dr. Oakden's figures for our poem into percentages, to facilitate comparison. I also quote in terms of percentages his figures for doublets and triplets (i.e. sets of two and three lines respectively with the same alliterating sound) in both poems. The following table results:

	S.	Q.
aaa/aa	4·9	0·3
aa/aa	46	7·2
aa/bb, ab/ba, ab/ab	1	19
aa/xx	1·3	14
xx/aa	0	6·6
doublets	7·4	3·5
triplets	0·5	0

In *The Quatrefoil of Love* there are several examples of the grouping of lines by part-alliteration, i.e. the alliterating sound of the second half of a line being carried over into the next line. This grouping device is a rather striking feature of our poem which in this respect affords another contrast with *The Pistill of Susan*.

Introduction

From the above figures it is evident that there is much difference in the use of alliteration in the two poems, *The Pistill of Susan* showing a greater tendency to excessive alliteration than our poem. Even when allowance has been made for the more complex subject-matter of *The Quatrefoil of Love*, the difference is a notable one.

A comparison of the rimes of the two poems yields the following results:

I. OE. $\bar{a}$: *ai*.
    Q. *maste* : *trayste* : *gaste* : *chaste* (xi).
    S. none.

II. OE., ON. $\bar{a}$ remain.
    Q. *care* : *sare* (ii); *sare* : *þare* : *mare* (xxxviii); *sare* : *ȝare* (xix); *hatte* : *late* (xxx).
    S. *sare* : *care* : *bare* : *ȝare* (xviii); *sore* : *wore* : *clare* : *mare* (xiv); *raþe* : *baþe* (xxvii).

III. OE., ON. $\bar{a}$: open $\bar{o}$.
    Q. *trone* : *one* (vii); *scorde* : *recorde* : *lorde* (xxxii).
    S. *wone* : *trone* : *one* : *none* (v); *hored* : *rored* : *lord* : *acorde* (xxvii).
    ON. $\bar{a}$: close $\bar{o}$.
    Q. *fonne* : *sone* (xxviii).
    S. none.

IV. close $\bar{e}$: open $\bar{e}$.
    Q. *stede* : *hede* : *reede* : *dede* (ii).
    S. *swere* : *here* (xiii); *deue* : *leue* (OE. *lēaf*) : *mischeue* : *forȝiue* (xix).

V. $\bar{e}$: i in open syllables.
    Q. *swete* : *wete* (i).
    S. *deue* : *leue* : *mischeue* : *forȝiue*[1] (xix) (?).

VI. $\bar{o}$: u in open syllables.
    Q. none.[2]
    S. *comes* : *domes* : *gomes* (iii).

VII. $\breve{y}$ ($\breve{u}$) : $\breve{\imath}$.
    Q. *begyn* : *kyn* : *syn* (xxxvii); *atyre* : *fyre* : *syre* : *hyre* (xxxiii).
    S. *wyre* : *fyre* : *schire* (xv).

[1] Köster may be right in rejecting this as a false reading, though the form with *i* is found in four out of the five MSS., the fifteenth-century MS. P being the exception.

[2] In *soꝩ* : *wone* : *trone* : *one* (vii), *u* appears to rime with open $\bar{o}$; compare the rime of open and close $\bar{o}$ in *fonne* : *sone* (xxviii). But more probably the rime here is u : u : $\bar{\rho}$: $\bar{\rho}$, to be compared with *Eue* : *bileue* : *belyue* : *stryue* (viii), where we have the rime $\bar{\imath}$: $\bar{\imath}$: $\bar{\imath}$: $\bar{\imath}$.

Introduction

VIII. $\bar{e} + j$ has become $\bar{\imath}$, and rimes with pure $\bar{\imath}$.
   Q. *hey* : *trye* : *crye* : *dye* (xv) ; *I* : *gentry* : *hye* : *wry* (xxxvii).
   $\bar{e} + h$ has remained $\bar{e}$, and rimes with pure $\bar{e}$.
   S. *tre* : *se* (1st s. pret.) : *ne* : *þre* (xxv) ; *tre* : *se* (2nd s. pret.) xxvi ;
   sene : *eyene* : *clene* (xxi).
IX. Final *e* is mute.
   Q. *blode* : *ȝode* (xvii) ; *all* : *calle* : *salle* : *haulle* (ix) ; *grett* : *mett* :
   lett : *sett* (xi) ; *wighte* : *lighte* : *myghte* (x) ; *solde* : *wolde* : *bolde* :
   tolde (xv).
   S. *blode* : *stode* (xxii); *place* : *face* : *case* : *wase* (xxvi); *feete* : *mete* (xx).
X. Final syllables are strong.
   Q. *I* : *gentry* (xxxvii) ; *by* : *lady* (xvii).
   S. *sage* : *lynage* : *langage* : *message* (ii) ; *alan* : *Susan* (iv) ; *cri* : *ladi*
   (xii).

From the above analysis it is evident that the outstanding differences between the rimes of the two poems appear under I and VIII. In VIII we note the raising of $\bar{e}$ + palatal to $\bar{\imath}$ in our poem, whereas it remains $\bar{e}$ in *The Pistill of Susan*. This is an important difference, pointing to a stronger Midland influence on the language of our text. With regard to I, there is only one example of the rime of OE. $\bar{a}$ with *ai* in the 520 lines of *The Quatrefoil of Love*, so that its non-occurrence in the 366 lines of *The Pistill of Susan* may be a mere coincidence. Other differences appear under III, VI, and perhaps V.

Vocabulary. An examination of the vocabularies of both *The Pistill of Susan* and *The Quatrefoil of Love* shows that the author of the former poem had a fuller vocabulary at his command. This is partly, but not altogether, to be explained by the larger number of synonyms he employs, as the following examples will illustrate :

For *man* we find the following :
   S. *mon, berne, barn, cherl, faunt, foode, gome, renke, segge, seneke, ȝouthe*, as well as *child*, in the sense of 'a grown-up person, usually male', though here applied to Susan.
   Q. *man, gedlynges.*

For *learning* or *knowledge* :
   S. *clergye, lair* (MSS. P and I), *lettrure, witand.*
   Q. *conynge, lare.*

For adjectives denoting *strength* and *nobility* :
   S. *borlich, dere, derf, fre, frelich, gentil, honest, honorablest, kene, maisterful, miȝti, real, worly.*

b

Q. *bolde, dere, dewe, fre, galiarde* (?), *gentil, ryalle.*
For *garden*:
S. *gardin, erber, erberi, orchard, pomeri, ȝarde.*
Q. *orcherde.*
For *beautiful*:
S. *auenaunt, briht, cleer, comelich, feire, louelich, louesum, schaply, schire, schene, semeli, swete, wlonkest.*
Q. *brighte, clere, comly, faire, lufly, schaply, semly, swete.*

Apart from this difference in fullness of vocabulary, there is also a difference in the actual words used by the two authors.

Amours, in his *Scottish Alliterative Poems*, 1897, has made a list of rare and remarkable words common to *The Pistill of Susan* and the alliterative *Morte Arthure*. They are: *bitok*, 'delivered', *bouwed*, 'went', *carped*, 'spoke', *child*, 'grown-up person', *clergye, eschewe, flayre, fodemed, foode*, 'person', *frelich*, 'noble', *gome*, 'person', *herbergages, kinrede, loselle, middelert, pomeri, rancour, rone, schawe, segge*, 'man', *selcouth*, 'marvellous', *sixti*, 'a large number', *stoteyd, trayle, trine*, 'to go', *wonde for*, 'to hesitate on account of', *winlich, ȝaply*. Of these twenty-eight words, only three appear in *The Quatrefoil of Love*, and these: *carpe, kynredyn, medilerthe*, are among the least remarkable. The following unusual words found in *The Quatrefoil of Love* do not occur in *The Pistill of Susan*: *belde to*, 'construct', *birde*, 'girl', *denyvs*, 'disdainful', *felauchip*, 'companion', *mellarse*, 'disputers'.

The alliterative expressions and stock phrases and epithets of the two poems also show a difference. We find the following alliterative tags and set expressions in *The Pistill of Susan* [1]: *bi se nor bi sande; þou sette vppon seuene; wiþ-inne the sercle of sees; þis dai ar we dine; þei cauȝt þe cursyng of kai; dampned on deis; in þe dismale; gladen and glees; for sert of hir souureyn;* **caste of hir kelle; in word ne in werk; in elde ne in ȝouthe;* **hedde cast of hir calle and hire keuercheue; bi norþ ne bi souþ; þat freoly foode; don out of dawen; most is of miht; nikke hem with nai; þat teeld is in trone; selcouþ to sene; wiþ tonge and wiþ top; þe wrong and þe riht; I charge hit not a pere; stoteyd and stode; bales to brewe; feole ferlys hire bi-felle; bi midday or none;* **wrong handes, iwis, and wepten wel sore; so lele in his lawe; preised als peere; proudest in pres; bretenet and brent; toret* (?)

[1] A star against an expression in *The Pistill of Susan* denotes a similar expression in *The Quatrefoil of Love*, and vice versa.

Introduction

and teone; renkes reneyed; worly in wone; at a mase; Iustises on bench; wlonkest in weede; *now waknep heor wo; louesum of lere; hende, ȝe mai here; of dedes so dere; so semeliche to siht; *siked wel sare˙; so mote þou þe; tristi and trewe; richest on rone; *schaply and schire; þe faunt, freli of face; no wonder, I wene; hir kinrede, hir cosyns; *to play; as well as stop-gap phrases : *þat day; *soþely to say; so tiht; in fay; no lees; so sone; in feere; *in drede; for soþ; nouht layne; in wede; withouten eni drede.

In *The Quatrefoil of Love* we find the following alliterative and set expressions : *rafe scho hir kertchefs, hir kelle of hir hede; *kelles and corchyfes; *wrange scho hir handis and wepe þan for wa; *on my playing; *schaply and schynand; mi wo and my wandrethe; within and with-owte; treson and tray; faire [of ?] face; stode in þat stede; þi speche and þi spelle; merie medilerthe; felawe and fere; to herken and to here; with buke and with belle; blenke of his blee; of mare and of myn; so trewe for to trayste; in hyde and in hewe; his body, his bone and his blode; fele famen; þe welthe of þis werlde; gamen and glewe; so meke and so mylde; so dewe ne so dere; of coloure so clere; cares will scho kele; bales may blyn; our flesche and our felle; wondis wyde; schynede and schane; *syghys þou so sare; wytter and wyde; to ryne and to ryde; no wrenke ne no wyle; no kythe ne no kyn; be lordis and be ladys; *to wakken oure waa; un-to wele or to wa; þe bonde and þe free; of lawe and of lare; I kane say ȝow na mare; þe sothe es noghte for to layne; grete dole for to see; blyssede mot scho be; grett ... and grym; and of stop-gap phrases : with-owtten any dowte; with-owtten any lett; *a sothe for to say; so ȝare; full ȝare; als I bileue; so still; as þay wolde; in hy; ful euyn; bot fonne; *þat day; so hende; *with drede.

From these lists it is evident that there is little resemblance between the set expressions of the two poems, and that those of *The Pistill of Susan* are more striking and, especially when we consider the different lengths of the two works, more numerous than those of *The Quatrefoil of Love*. Judging by the vocabulary, the author of the first-mentioned poem is a more literary man, with a larger and richer vocabulary and a larger and richer supply of literary phrases at his command, than the author of our poem.

Style. There is a marked difference in style between the two poets. Both show a gift of narrative, the story in each case being told simply and directly, and working up well from its beginning to its conclusion. There are two minor exceptions to the steady onward flow of the narrative in our poem; at the beginning of stanza xii and again of stanza xviii, the author has to go back in his story to pick up the thread of his narrative. In *The Pistill of Susan*, the poet holds up the action to give us, through four stanzas, an elaborate and rather quaint description of Joachim's garden. In spite of this, we feel that, for the author of *The Pistill of Susan*, the story and the people in it are of paramount importance, whereas in *The Quatrefoil of Love* the narrative is only the vehicle for the moral and the characters are mere lay figures. The author is a moralist casting his sermon in the form of a story to make his teaching attractive, whereas the poet of *The Pistill of Susan* is more of a conscious artist, interested in the story for its own sake, and showing a sensitiveness to natural beauty and a genuine sympathy with his characters. Susan is a real person and we are made to feel the attraction of her beauty; 'þis loueliche ladi' is 'louelich and lilie-whit'; she is 'þis schaply þing', 'semeli Susan', and 'þat ladi louesum of lere'. The Biblical passage which describes her, to use the Wycliffite version, as 'ful delicate, and faire of fourme', the poet has expanded to:

> 'Hir hed was ȝolow as wyre
> Of gold fyned wiþ fyre,
> Hire scholdres schaply and schire
> þat bureliche was bare.'

No opportunity is missed of making a picture of her:

> 'Heo com with two Maidens, al richeli þat day,
> In riche robus arayed, red as þe rose',

and in the judgement-hall she appears,

> 'In a selken schert, with scholdres wel schene'.

The two elders also are real people; we can see them with their 'hor heuedus', and with their cumbersome cloaks impeding their progress as they 'trinet a trot', so they said, after Susan and her imaginary lover; or with 'chekes wel pale' when Daniel, with dramatic directness, attacks first one, then the other:

> 'Þou dotest nou on þin olde tos in þe dismale.'

Even Susan's two maid-servants are given their names, Sibyl and Joan, and Joachim reaches almost heroic proportions in the beautiful farewell scene:

Introduction

> 'And euere he cussed þat swete:
> "In oþer world schul we mete."
> Seid he no mare.'

The dramatic pathos of this scene, the sense of beauty shown throughout the work, and the feeling for character betoken the poet. So too does the love of pictorial effect shown in such descriptions as that of Joachim's house on a wooded height surrounded by a moat, or in the elaborate account of his garden with its trees, birds, fruits, flowers, and vegetables. Neither is there any direct moralizing, the story with its dramatic and poetical possibilities is what matters to the author.

With *The Quatrefoil of Love* it is another matter. True, we have the picture of the 'mery orcherde' with its brightly coloured 'blomes and blossomes', its well and its trees and birds, but little is made of this conventional medieval setting, only six lines in a poem of over 500 being devoted to the description of Nature. The opportunity of making a beautiful picture is here lost, as it is again when we are introduced to the girl. What do we know of her? Nothing, except her despair in the beginning at not finding a true-love and, in the end, her rather unconvincing acceptance of the turtle-dove's teaching. We do not know her name, we are told nothing of her appearance. The promise held out to us in:

> 'All my hert and my thoghte walde I þe telle,
> Mi wo and my wandrethe, walde þou come nere',

is not realized in the poem, for the turtle-dove almost immediately begins his sermon, and this occupies the rest of the poem except the last stanza, when we hear again of the girl:

> 'Thus this trewe turtyll techis this may,
> Scho blyssede his body, his bone and his blode.'

That is all; the rest of the stanza is occupied with the author, in his own person, stressing the moral of the turtle-dove's sermon. The girl is, in fact, nothing but a lay-figure on which to fasten the moral. Indeed, the turtle-dove quite early loses sight of her, for in line 75 he addresses a plural audience: 'Halde this lefe in ȝour mynde'. The lapse is significant; the author momentarily has forgotten his rôle of turtle-dove addressing the girl and has shown himself as he really is, a preacher addressing his congregation. In line 31 of *The Pistill of Susan* there is a lapse, similar but with a difference, for the author, who has hitherto been speaking in the third person, adds (no doubt, to complete the line): 'hende (i.e. gentle listeners), ȝe mai here', thereby betraying the literary man, the *scop* addressing his audience.

The turtle-dove, too, goes undescribed, in spite of his important rôle. Yet in *The Pistill of Susan* the unimportant birds in Joachim's garden are distinguished by name, and little pen pictures made of them: 'nihtyngales vppon nest', 'turtils troned on trene', 'þe popeiayes perken and pruynen for proude'.

The explanation of the difference is this: our author is telling the story of the Life and Passion of Christ, with the special object of exalting Mary. He uses the conventional framework of the *chanson d'aventure*, but does not dwell overmuch on it, thinking, no doubt rightly, that to do so would distract his audience from his main theme. Only in his descriptions of the spiritual personages in the drama do we catch some hint of a sense of beauty on his part: Gabriel is fair, Mary has 'eghne graye', she is 'þat swete wighte', 'þat bryghte'. Our author shows narrative and dramatic power, and also pictorial faculty in his description of the Last Judgement and the folk arraigned thereat and in his account of the Harrying of Hell, but he is moralist first and foremost.

Authorship and Date. Neither manuscript of *The Quatrefoil of Love* gives any indication of the authorship or date of the poem. From internal evidence it would appear firstly, that it is not by the same author as *The Pistill of Susan*, and secondly, that it was probably written by a cleric. The Vernon and Additional MSS. of *The Pistill of Susan* belong to the last third of the fourteenth century, and these obviously do not represent the original text. The composition of the poem has, by general consent, been assigned to the middle of the fourteenth century and there seems no good reason why *The Quatrefoil of Love* should not also belong to that period.

There is, as we have seen, some difference in the dialect and a marked difference in the use of alliteration, in the vocabulary, and in the literary style and outlook of the two poems, such as can only be explained by a difference of authorship. *The Pistill of Susan* appears to have been written by a poet and literary man of the world, whereas *The Quatrefoil of Love* would seem to be the work of a clerical moralist.

The Poem. *The Quatrefoil of Love* is interesting chiefly in its anthropomorphic aspect, throwing light, as it does, on certain phases of medieval mentality. Our poem is, in its framework, a medieval attempt at the sublimation of the sex instinct. A maiden whose heart is set on finding an earthly lover is taught by a turtle-dove to sublimate her human desire into the spiritual love for God and His Mother. The process, however, is not too skilfully carried out; little emphasis is laid on the supreme beauty and loveableness of the Spiritual Lover, and the ultimate appeal of the poem is to fear rather than to love. In this respect it invites comparison with the much finer *Luve Ron*, by Thomas of Hales, where the sublimation motif really is important and Christ is stressed as the Divine Lover. By its framework, then, our poem is linked to the great medieval debate between Sacred and Profane Love.

But the real object of the work is the glorification of the Mother of God, and the author uses a conventional literary form together with contemporary folk-lore to further his purpose. Very interesting, too, is the forensic conception of the Last Judgement, and the light it throws on medieval justice, the power of 'the queen', and the system of courtly patronage. The conception of the position of Mary is not consistent throughout the poem. At the beginning she is exalted into a fourth person of the Trinity, but she does not maintain this exalted position to the end. At the Last Judgement she is not, as in other medieval works, the imperious queen overriding the decrees of the judge, but rather the gentle suppliant whose prayers and bribes are unavailable against the stern justice of her Son. Mary is all-powerful (though chiefly through her tears and prayers) while we are in this life, but even she cannot save us at the last, if we neglect her help in this world—that is the final moral of the poem.

The conception of the next world as a place where the wrongs of the just are righted and their sufferings meet with reward is the heaven of the New Testament, but our medieval ancestors went further. Suffering and want are bearable when they are recognized as the inevitable portion of all, but 'how bitter a thing it is to look into happiness through another man's eyes'. So, in their conception of heaven, it was not enough for them to believe in their own ultimate reward for present suffering, but their crude sense of justice demanded the full swing of the pendulum, and those whose happier lot in this life had intensified by contrast their own sad fate must in their turn provide the dark foil to the joy of their reward in the next world. Hence the doctrine of the blessed rejoicing in the pains of the damned. Our author does not go nearly as far as that, but in stanzas xxxv–xxxvii we catch hints of this attitude towards the great ones of this earth.

Our poem also throws some light on the extravagance in dress and other abuses of the times, and on the clerical attitude towards them.

The four-leaved clover was not only, on account of its resemblance in form to a true-love knot and probably also because of its rarity, a symbol of faithful love, but it figures in folk-lore as an emblem of good luck generally. Its English association with a lover is illustrated in the old rhyme:

> 'If you find an even ash-leaf,
> Or a four-leaved clover,
> You'll be bound to see your true-love
> Ere the day be over.'

In Belgium, too, if it is plucked by a girl on the Eve of St. John, it brings her a husband. In Chaucer's *Miller's Tale*, the lover Absolon had a superstitious belief in its efficacy for, when on his way to court Alisoun,

> 'Under his tonge a trewe-love he beer,
> For ther-by wende he to ben gracious'.

Love, however, was not the only sphere in which the four-leaved clover brought luck. In the Vosges country it was very dangerous to attack the werewolf unless you were carrying this talisman about you without knowing it, for if you were not so protected your bullets, unless blessed in a chapel of St. Hubert, would merely rebound from the monster's back. In the Tyrol a four-leaved clover, gathered while the Vesper bell is ringing on Midsummer Eve, endows the gatherer with magical powers; in Saintonge and Aunis, if found on the Eve of St. John, it brings good luck at play.[1]

Just as St. Patrick, according to legend, found the three-leaved shamrock a useful device for explaining to his converts the doctrine of the Trinity, so the author of our poem found in the quatrefoil a means to the glorification of Mary, and basing his narrative on current folk-lore presented to his audience the claims of God and His Mother to be the only worthy objects of their love.

In conclusion, I wish to thank Dr. Mabel Day for reading the proofs of this edition, and for some helpful suggestions of which I have availed myself.

M. M. W.

---

[1] See Frazer's *The Golden Bough*, x. 316, xi. 62–3.

THE QUATREFOIL OF LOVE

I

IN a moruenyng of Maye wheñ Medowes saíf spryng [f. 98]
Blomes and blossomes of brighte colours,
Als I went by a welle on my playing,
Thurgh a mery orcherde bedande myñ hourres,
The birdis one bewes bi-gane for to synge,
And bowes for to burgeoñ and belde to þe bour[es],   6
Was I warre of a maye þat made mournyng,
Sekande and syghande amange þase floures
      So swete.
    Scho made mournynge ynoughe,
    Hir wepynge dide [me] woughe,
    Vndir a tree I me droughe,   12
    Hir wiíl walde I wete.

II

STILLY I stalkede and stode in þat stede,
For I walde wiete of hir wiíl and of hir wilde thoghte.
Rafe scho hir kertchefs, hir keíle of hir hede,
Wrange scho [hir] handis and wrothely scho wrog[hte];
Scho saide: 'mylde mary, righte þou me reede,   18
For of alle þe wele of þis werlde [i-wys] I welde [noghte],
Sende me somme socour or soune be I dede,
Som sight of þat selcouth þat I hafe lange soughte
      With care.'
    Thane spake a Turtiíl one a tree,
    With faire notis and free :   24
    'Thou birde for thi beaute,
    Whi syghys þou so sare?'

III

'A THOU, faire foule, faile noghte þi speche and þi spelle,
Thi carpyng es comforthe to herkeñ and to [here],
Aíl my hert and my thoghte walde I þe telle,
Mi wo and my wandrethe, walde þou come ner[e].'   30

3 on] B of.   11 A dide woughe : B dyde me rogh.   17 A scho handis : B scho hir handes.   19 A werlde I welde..,: B warlde I wys I walde noȝte.   28 A and to... : B and here.   29 hert] B wyíl.

B

Than lufly he lyghtede, walde he noghte duelle
To co*m*forthe þat comly *and* cou*er* hir chere.
Scho blyssede his body w*ith* buke *and* w*ith* belle,
And louede þat lady þat sente hir þat fere
   So fre.
 'When I was sary,   36
 Besoughte I oure lady,
 Scho hase sente me company,
   Blyssede mote scho bee.

IV

' THOU faire foulle full of lufe, so mylde *and* so swete,
 To moue of a mater now walde I be-gyn͂:
A trewe-lufe hafe I soughte be waye *and* be strete,   42
In many faire orcherdis *per* flou*r*es er I[n];
Als ferre als I hafe soughte I fande nane ȝitt,
Fele hafe [I] funden͂ of mare *and* of myn͂.
Brighte birde of þⁱ blee, my Balis may þou bete,
Wald þou me wysse weyssely a trewluf [to wyn͂]
   With reghte.   48
 When I wene ratheste
 For to fynde lufe beste,
 So feyntely es it feste,
   It fares alle on flyghte.'

V

' THE witte of a woman͂ es wonder to here,
 Es all þⁱ sare syghynge to seke lufe trewe?   54
Alle thi sythe may þou sighe *and* neu*er* mare be nere,
Bot if þou hade concelle of one þat I knewe,
Whare it es spryngande [*and*] eu*er*-more newe,
W*ith*owtten͂ diffady*n*ge, full faire *and* full clere,
Or castyng of coloure or changynge of hewe.
If þou be sett for to seke ȝit sall I þᵉ lere   60

39 A *scho* corrected to *he* written above it in a different hand, somewhat later
(? sixteenth century): B scho.   42 trewe-lufe] B trewful (with *ful* erased
and *luf* added after).   44 I fande] B fand*e* I.   45 A omits *I*: B haue I
fonden͂.   47 B to wyn͂: The edge of MS. A is damaged.   48 reghte] B
ryg....   55 Alle thi sythe may þou sighe] B Al þis syd may þou seke.   57 A
spryngande eu*er*-more; B spryngand*e and* eu*er*-more.

An Alliterative Religious Lyric

  So ʒare.
Hardely dare I say
Ther is no l[u]f þat lastis ay,
With-owtten tresoñ *and* tray,
  Bot if it bygyñ thare.

VI   [f. 98 v.]

WHARE þou fyndis grewande a trewlufe grysse, 66
 W*ith* iiij [lefes] es it sett full louely aboute.
The firste lefe we may lykeñ vn-to þᵉ kynge of blisse,
Þat weldis alle þis werlde w*ith*-iñ *and* w*ith*-owte;
He wroghte heueñ w*ith* his hande *and* alle paradise,
And þis merie medilerthe w*ith*-owtteñ any dowte;
Alle þᵉ welthe of þ*is* werlde hally is his, 72
In whaṁ vs awe for to leue, loue hym *and* lowtte
  Full wele.
Halde this lefe in ʒo*ur* mynde,
Till we † his felawes fynde,
Of þat trewlufe *and* þat kynde,
  Þat neu*er*-more sall kele. 78

VII

NOW bi this ilk seconde lefe I likeñ goddis soñ,
 Vn-to þ*is* ilke firste lefe es felawe and fere;
The thirde vn-to þᵉ holy gaste, to-gedir [þay w]one;
Þase iij leues are of price w*ith*-owtteñ any pere.
Wheñ þat semly kynge es sett on his trone,
Comly of coloure, curtase and clere, 84
Es no-thynge in this werlde lyke to hy*m* one;
His gladenesse *and* his gudnesse comforthes vs here
  Off grace.
Alle this werlde he by-gane,
W*ith* wynde *and* † wat*er* wanne,
And sythen he makede mane, 90
  After his awenñ Face.

63 A lyf(e): B luf. 67 A iiij es: B iiij le*fes* is. 73 leue loue] B lefe *and* loue. 75 ʒo*ur*] B þⁱ. 76 A Till we may his: B To we his. 77 B omits *Of*. 79 Now bi] B By. 81 A are done: B þay woñ. 84 coloure curtase and clere] B colo*ur and* curtas of chere. 89 A w*ith* wat*er*: B omits *with*. 90 B And syne made he mañ.

VIII

FIRSTE made he Adam and sythen made he Eue,
Putt he þam in paradisse in full grete degree,
Forbede he þam no-thynge, als I bileue,
Bot a grene appille þat grew one a tree.
Bot þan sary sathanasse soughte þam belyue,   96
For to wakken oure waa, þer weryede mott he bee,
Toke þam þat appill to stirre mekill stryue ;
Þe foule fende was fayne þat syghte for to see
    For tene.
  Þe firste lefe was full woo,
  When his floures felle hym froo,   102
  His frendys solde to helle goo,
    For a nappill grene.

IX

ÞAN bigan þe firste lefe to morne for vs all,
For his lufly handwerke þat he hade lorne.
Gabriel þat aungelle on hym gun he calle ;
Forthe come þat semely and knelde hym bi-forne.   108
'Goo to mayden Marie, my messagere, þou salle,
And bere hir blythe bodworde, of hir will I be borne.'
Þus he sent his dere sone owt of his heghe haulle,
Vn-to þat mylde mayden in a mery morne,
    And hir grett.
  Gabriel, þat faire face,   114
  Haylsede Marie full of grace,
  Sayde, 'pereles in alle place,
    With myrthe arte þou mett.

X

'ÞOU sall consayue a knaue childe comly and clere,
And all þe bale of þis werlde in þe sall be bett.'
'Þat were a mekill meruelle þat I a childe solde bere, 120
Was I neuer maryede ne with man mett.'

93 B Putt þam. 97 B omits þer. mott] B myȝt. 106 B For lufe
of hys handwarke þat þan was lorn. 109-110 B Vnto mayden mary my
message þou schall Bere hir bodworde of hire I wyll be born. 112 in] B on.
115-16 B Sayd mary full of grace Pereles in ilka place. 120 þat I &c.] B
I sulde a cheld bere.

An Alliterative Religious Lyric

' Be-halde to thi Cosyn̄, consayuede hase to-ȝere
Elezebeth in hir [e]lde, þat lange hase bene l[ett].'
' Lorde, thi hande-mayden̄,' said Marie, 'es here,
Full hally in thi seruyce es my hert sett
    So still.'   126
Blissede be þat swete wighte,
That God sone in̄ lighte,
Be-come man̄ full of myghte,
    With his Fadir will.

XI

NOW þis ilk secounde lefe, for [owr] lufe maste, [f. 99.]
   Lighte in [þat lady] þat gabryel grett,   132
W*ith*-owtten̄ any *t*reson̄ so trewe for to trayste,
W*ith* myrthe i*n* a mayden̄ es god *and* man̄ mett.
It es þᵉ Fadir *and* þᵉ sone *and* þᵉ haly gaste,
Thre leues of lufe w*ith*-owtten̄ any lett,
Þᵉ ferthe es þᵉ mayden̄ chosen̄ for chaste,
Swilk anoþ*er* trewlufe was neu*er* i*n* lande sett   138
    For bote.
Thies foure leues maye neu*er* falle,
Bot eu*er*-more þay sprynge sall,
So gentill þay joyne alle
    One a righte rote.

XII

NOW † thies [iij] louely leues a f[ourte fela] hase tane, 144
   For lufe in oure lady es oure lorde [lyghte],
Josephe hir weddede *and* w*ith* hir gonn̄ gane,
In þᵉ burghe of bedlem̄ beldede þat bryghte,
By-twix an Oxe *and* an Asse, pride was þare nane,
A blyssede barne was þ*er* borne appon̄ a ȝole [nyȝte];
There rasse a sterne hastily þ*at* schynede and schane, 150
   III kynges of Coloyne þ*er*of hade [a] sight[e],

123 B held. B lett. 131 Now þis] B Now is þis. A for lufe : B for owr luf.
132 A a mayden̄ : B þat lady. 133 trayste] B treste. 140 MS. *thre* erased
and *foure* substituted. 142 B gently þai grewyn̄. 144 A Now all thies foure
louely leues a frende to þam̄ hase tane : B Now has þer iij leues a fourte fela tan̄.
145 B lyght. 149 a ȝole . . .]: B þᵉ ȝole nyȝte. 150 hastily] B schaply.
schynede] B schewed. 151 a] A þay : B a.

And soughte.
Þay offerde to hym, as þay wolde,
Mirre, Rekills, and Golde,
He thankkede þam͡ fele-folde,
  To blysse he þam͡ broghte.   156

XIII

VNSELY Herawde þis tythynges herde telle,
  Þat a [knaw] childe was borne þat kyng scholde be,
Garte he make message and sent he full snelle
To seke ✝ knaue childe[r] in þat cite.
Lefte he nane in qwarte bot alle gan͡ he quelle ;
Þay spetide þam͡ one speris, grete dole for to see.   162
Josephe with his wedde wyffe walde noghte duelle,
He led hir in-to Egippe with hir leues three
  To saue.
Thase childre gane theire dede take,
For þat same trewlufe sake,
The mare myrthe may þay make,   168
  Hym-selfe walde þam͡ haue.

XIV

3ITT walde he mare do for his frendis dere,
  For his haly hande-werke to helle walde he ga[ne] ;
To sett vs ensample his lay for to lere,
Saynt John Baptiste hym in flom jordane ;
For thritty penys was he saulde thurgh a false fere, 174
Vn-to fele famen͡ þat fayne walde hym [hafe slane] ;
All he sufferde for oure syn͡, hym-selfe was clere,
Thurgh a kysse þay hym knewe and tytte wa[s he tane]
  Also.
It was grete dole for to see,
When he scholde blenke of his blee,   180
Þe secund lefe of þe three,
  Þe ferthe was wo.

153 to hym] B him͡.   155 fele-folde] B VII folde.   157 B þase tythandes.
158 A childe : B knaw chylde.   160 A to seke þat knaue childe etc. : B To seke
knafe chylder in þat contre.   167 B For þer (altered from þat) trewluf sake.
173 B hym baptyste.

XV

PILATE was Justice and satt appoñ hey,
For to deme Jh*es*u þat Judas hade solde;
He said, 'leue lordynges, a treuthe for to trye,
Þ*a*t semely es saklesse, say what 3e wold[e].'   186
The Jewes appoñ Jh*es*u bigane for to crye,
'He said hy*m*selfe he es a kynge, slyk wordis are [bolde],
And if þou wiff noghte deme hy*m* þis day for to dye,
Ryghte bifore [þ*e*] Emp*er*our þ*is* tale saff be to[lde],
      For dred[e].'
A drery dome gaffe he thare,   192
I kane say 3ow na mare,
' I rede þat 3e take hy*m* [3]are,
And forthe 3e hym lede.'

XVI

ALLAS for þ*a*t ferthe lefe was lefte þan allañ,
When hir faire felauchip was taken *and* [torne],
Betyñ w*ith* scowrges, body and bane,   198
Sythyñ sprede one a crosse *and* crownned w*ith* thor[ne];
Thurgh his handis and his fete þ*e* nayles gañ gane,   [f. 99 v.]
A bygg spere tiff his hert brathely was borne;
He schede his blode for oure lufe, leued he hy*m* nane,
Attir and ayseff þay bedde hy*m* for skorne,
      With [g]affe.   204
It was gret dole for to see,
When he was naylede one a tree,
Þ*e* seconde lefe of þ*e* three
      Sulde falowe and faffe.

XVII.

THE ferthe lefe of þ*a*t trewlufe allanly scho stode,
Wrange scho hir handis *and* wepe þan for wa,   210
W*ith* a mou*r*nande chere and w*ith* a drery mode.
Þ*e* sou*n*e blenkede of his ble *and* wexe þañ aff bla,

188 B says.   B bald.   190 A bifore Emp*er*our: B befoŕ þ*e* Emp*er*owre.
B tald*e*.   194 A þare: B yar*e* (?=3ar*e*).   197 B torñ.   199 B w*ith*
a thorñ.   200 B goñ gañ.   204 A With affe: B W*ith* gaff.   205
It was gret dole for] B Grett reuth was.   209 þat trewlufe] B þ*e* lufe.   210 A
scho wrange: B Wrange scho.

Be his white sydes rane þe rede blode,
Þe harde roche gane ryue þe temple in twa,
Þan swounede þat ferthe lefe *and* to þe grounde ȝode.
Allas for þat trew-lufe þat it sulde twynͩ swa, 216
  So ȝare.
Scho sawe hir dere sonͩ dy,
[Bot] sayn John was by,
And comforthede þat lady,
  Was castenͩ in care.

XVIII

Þ AN spak þat noble kynge was naylede on þat tre, 222
Vn-tiH his modir dere was mo*ur*nande þat tyde :
' Leue þⁱ wepynge, womanͩ, *and* morne noghte for me,
Take John to þⁱ sonͩ þat standis bi þⁱ syde ;
John, take mary [m]ⁱ moder now [moder] to þe,
To kepe *and* to comforthe, ȝoure blysse for to byde.'
Þe hate blode of his hert dide longeus to see, 228
Þat rane by þ• spere-schafte fra his wondis wyde
  Þat daye.
It was grete dole for to se,
When he was taken of þe tre,
Þe seconde lefe of the three
  Was closede in claye. 234

XIX

W HEN he was dede on þe rode *and* dolvenͩ so ȝare,
AH þe welthe of þ*i*s werlde in thre leues it lay,
Þe ferthe lefe þanͩ falowede *and* syghede fuH sare,
† AH þe trewthe of þ*i*s werlde was i*n* a trewe may.
Þof his manhed ware dede his myghtis was þ• mare,
Appon his haly ha*n*dwerk was his he*r*t ay ; 240
Þe saule w*it*h þe godhede to helle ganͩ þay fare,
Þe body w*it*h þe manhede habade þ^e thirde day

---

219 A And : B Bot.   was by] B was hir by.   222 Þan] B ȝitt.   226 A
þⁱ moder now to þ^e : B to þⁱ mod*er* mary to þ^e.   227 B ȝo*ur* blys to a-byde.
229 This and the previous line are out of place in A at the beginning of the
stanza.   237 lefe] B fela.   238 A *and* aH : B Al   239 Þof] B If.   myghtis] B
myȝte.

An Alliterative Religious Lyric

   Full ȝare.
Þat he hade w*ith* his handis wroghte,
And sythen w*ith* his blude boghte,
Till þay were owt of balis broghte,   246
   Hym langede full sare.

XX

THAN said ⸵ sary Sathanas, his sorowe was full sade,
 For [s]ight of þat selcouth he wexe al vn-fayne:
'Vs co*m*mes som bodworde, I hope it be badde.
What art þou w*ith* þⁱ fare?' faste goñ he frayne.
'Kynge of joy es my name, þⁱ gestis for to glade,   252
Late me in for þaire lufe, now thare the nogte layne.'
'Wende away w*ith* þⁱ myrthe, þou makis me all made,
What solde þou do i*n* þ*i*s pitt, þou sees here bot payñ
   So faste.'
   When þay herde þ^e kynge speke,
   Alle þ^e ȝatis gañ þay steke,   258
   Bot soñ gañ þ^e bandis breke,
   And alle þ^e barres braste.

XXI

FOR his haly handwerke heried he helle,
 And all broghte he owte of bale þat eu*er* hade bene his;
Dauyd, his derlynge, made myrthe þ*er* emelle,
He tuk an harpe i*n* his hande *and* weldide it iwysse;   264
And all his retenewe owte gonñ he telle,
And for his grete m*er*cy for-gaffe þa*m* þair mysse:
'I was saulde for ȝo*ur* sake *and* sufferde wondis felle,
And all my boñ childir are broghte vn-to blysse,
   On rode.'
   Þ^e sothe es noghte for to layne,   [f. 100.] 270
   When þay were broghte owt of payne,
   Vn-to þ^e body a-gayne
   Þ^e haly gaste ȝode.

244 B hand. 246 B bale. 248 A said þat sary: B sayd sary. was full sade] B wex sad*e*. 249 A light: B syght. 250 hope] B trow. 253 now thare the nogte] B thar þou noȝte. 263 þ*er* emelle] B þ*er* of I mell. 264 B *and* well he dyd I wys. 267 felle] B snell. 268 B gud chyld*er*.

XXII

Þᴇ ferthe lefe of þat trewlufe falowede for waa,
Whan scho was leuede modir, Mayden and wyfe.
Þᵉ fyrste lefe full of myghte his will was swa, 276
By assent of þᵉ thirde lefe was þer no stryfe,
Raysede þay þᵉ seconde lefe by-twixe þam twa,
Thrugh grace of þᵉ godhede fra dede vn-to lyfe.
He toke þᵉ crose in his hande and forthe gon he ga,
With his flesche and his felle and his wondis fyve,
    He ȝode. 282
When he was rysen agayne,
He mett with þe Maudelayne,
Na ferly if scho were fayne,
    He was hir leche gude.

XXIII

Fᴏʀᴛʜᴇ ȝode þᵉ Maudelayne with myrthe in hir mode,
Tolde scho thies tythynges to thomas of [ynde]: 288
'Criste es resyn alle hale þat schede his hert blode,
Trow now þis, tomas, þou sall it sothe fynde.'
And þan spake thomas in stede þer he stode:
'Women are † carp[and], it commes þam of kynde',
Walde he neuer leue it þat criste hym-selfe ȝode,
Or he appered to þᵉ appostills, as clerkes hase in [mynde], 294
    In hy.
He putt his hande in his syde,
And alle he blyssed in þat tyde,
Þat leuede in his wondis wyde,
    And sawe þam neuer with ey.

XXIV

Fᴏʀᴛʜᴇ wente þat semely, a sothe for to say, 300
He ȝode to his discypills and taghte þam trewthe t[rewe],
And sythen to þat lady þat he louede ay,
Alle hale of his hurtes in hyde and in hewe ;

---

274 trewlufe] B lufe.   288 B ynde.   292 A of carpynge : B carpaṅd.
293 þat] B or.   294 B omits Or he. A first two strokes of m visible : B mynde.
300 a] B þᵉ.   301 ȝode to] B soght.   A long stroke of r visible after t :
B trew.

An Alliterative Religious Lyric

Scho was stabill *and* still *and* faylede neue*r* fay,
Þase foure leues of lufe sprynges all new[e],
Oure lorde steghe i*n*-till heueñ one halowe thoresday, 306
Sythen folowed his mod*er* wit*h* gamen [*and*] glew[e],
   Ful euyñ.
Bifore hir sone scho knelyd douñ,
W*ith* full gude deuocyouñ,
Vp-on hir hede he sett a crouñ,
   And made hir qwen of heuen. 312

XXV

Þ<small>E</small> ferthe lefe of þ*at* trewlufe, blyssede mot scho be!
Scho may hafe joy i*n* hir h*er*t of hir ge*n*til chi[ld],
Appon his fadir right hand hir soñ may scho see,
And þ*e* hende haly gaste vn-to þa*m* bathe b[elde].
Now are þay samen i*n* a gode, þase p*er*sou*n*s
And scho es maydeñ of myght *and* modyr ful myl[de]; 318
Swilk anoþ*er* trewlufe grew neue*r* on tre,
Wha-so leues i*n* þ*er* lufe sall neue*r* be bi-gyled,
   So hende.
Bot wele es þat ilk wyghte,
Þat may be sekir of þat syghte,
Þer eue*r* es day *and* neue*r* nyghte, 324
   And joye wit*h*-owtten ende.

XXVI

Þ<small>US</small> hase this faire trewlufe made vs all fre,
Our saules owt of bondage he boghte [on þ*e* rode],
He coma*n*dis vs for to kepe, *and* giffes vs pouste,
O*ur* saules out of syñ for o*ur* aweñ gude.
Mekill sorow wolde we hafe myght we o*ur* saulles see, 330
When þay ar sounkeñ i*n* syñ as fer[cost] in fl[ode],
For þan bide we i*n* bonddage i*n* bale for to be,
Þat he hase boghte hally wit*h* his hert [blode]

---

307 A *and* is illegible; MS. cut at edge: B *and* wit*h* glew. 313 trewlufe] B lufe. 314 B chyld*e*. 316 A *gl* erased, and *b* und traces of *e* are written below: B beld*e*. 318 B myld*e*. 319 trewlufe] B trewfull. 324 Þer] B Whar. 326 B trewfull. 327 B on þ*e* rode. 331 B farcost in flode. 333 A hert...: B awñ blod*e*.

To blysse.
Aske mercy whills we may,
Bot oure lady for vs pray,   336
Or we be closede in clay,
Off myrthe may we mysse.

XXVII

BLYSSEDE be þat trewlufe so meke *and* so mylde,
Sekir *and* stedfaste *and* stabill at assaye;
When we hafe wrethede *per* thre leues w*ith* our werkes wilde,
Þe ferthe es gr*a*cious *and* gude for to helpe aye.   342
Þan kneles þat lady dowñ bi-fore hir dere childe,
And sare wepys for our sake w*ith* hir eghne graye;
Scho es eu*er* full of gr*a*ce, † ells were we by-gylede,
Scho wȳnnes w*ith* hir wepynge many faire praye
        To kepe.
    Sen scho es welle of oure wele,   348
    And alle oure cares will scho kele,
    Allas, whi gare we hir knele,
    And for oure werkes wepe!

XXVIII

NOW es no wighte in þis werlde so dewe ne so dere,
No kyng ne no kayser þof þay bere crowñ,
Ne non so faire lady of coloure so clere,   354
Bot co*m*mes dredefull dede *and* drawes þa*m* dowñ;
Vs liste neu*er* leue it for preste ne for frere,
Or we fele þat we falle we swelte *and* we swouñ,
Bot wheñ our bare body es broghte one a bere,
Þan failes alle felawchipe in felde *and* in towññ,
        Bot fonne.   360
    In a clathe are we knytt,
    And sytheñ putt in a pytt,
    Of alle þ*is* werlde are we qwitt,
        For-getyñ are we sone.

---

339 B trewfull, with *full* erased and *luf* written above.   340 at assaye] B in faye.   345 A gr*a*ce *and* ells : B gr*a*ce els.   346 wȳnnes] so A : B wȳnes.   352 dewe] B derñ.   356 A liste vs : B Vs lyst.   357 we swelte etc.] B w*ith* swelt or w*ith* swone.   360 B fone.

XXIX

Bot for þat kaytefde corse es fuȝȝ littiȝȝ care,
And we be sekir of our saule were þat we saȝȝ duelle; 366
Bot now no wyghte in þis werlde so wyse es of lare,
No clerke bi his conynge þat þer-of kañ telle,
How felle wayes ne how ferre vs falles for to fare,
Bot harde wayes are to heueñ and hasty to heȝȝe;
In purgatorye es payne who-so commes þer,
Of mekiȝȝ wa may þay wytt þat þer-in saȝȝ dueȝȝe 372
    Fuȝȝ lange.
  Þat we do are we fare,
  Bi-fore vs fynde we fuȝȝ ȝare,
  We may be sekir of na mare,
    When Paynes are so strange.

XXX

When grett fyres and gryɱ are graythede in oure gate, 378
  Þer es no glasyng by, bot Iñ buse vs glyde;
When we are putt in þat payne so harde and so hatte,
We seeke after socoure on euerylke a syde,
We calle on oure kynredyñ, þay comme alle to late,
Wheñ we hafe frayste of þat fare, felde es our pride;
Bot þan [of] aȝȝe our sorowe na certayne ende we wate, 384
Bot triste in a trewelufe his mercy to byde,
    With drede.
  Bot now were tyme to by-gyñ,
  Þat trewlufe for to wyñ,
  Þat aȝȝ oure bales may blyñ,
    Wheñ we hafe maste nede. 390

XXXI

Of alle þe dayes þat we hafe drede ȝit awe vs to knawe,
  When we vmthynke vs of ane, fuȝȝ sare may we gryse;
Þat gret lorde and þat gryɱ when his bemys saȝȝ blawe,
And þe hey iustys saȝȝ sytt apon a ful gret sysse,

---

366 B And we ware sykere of owr sales ware we schulde dweȝȝ. 369 B How feȝȝ ne how fayr. 370 B harde way is. 375 B we yare. 379 B gladynge. 381 B euer ilka syde. 382 B kynrede. 384 of] A es: B is. B omits ende. 385 B to a-byde. 391 B days we haue to drede. 394 B And þat hy justyse saȝȝ syte in his syse.

And alle þe folke of þis werlde saƚƚ ryse on a Rawe,
Þan þe qwik, may qwake, when þe dede sal vp-rysse.   396
We may lett for no chance oure synnes for to schewe,
Þer may no golde ne no fee make oure maynpryce,
  No kyn.
Þan es aƚƚ our pryde gane,
Oure robis *and* our riche pane,
Alle bot a crysome [al]ane,   402
  Þat we were crystened In.

XXXII

WHEN we are callede to þat count bi-houes vs to here,
  Þer aƚƚ saƚƚ be soyttures, bothe þe bonde *and* þe free,
Þe sauƚƚ[es] [*and* þ]e bodyes þat lan[g]e ha[s]e bene se[r]e,
Þam [behou]es samen come vn-to þat semelye ;
Ilk a saule saƚƚ be sent at fett hys awenn fere, [f. 101.]   408
When cryst wiƚƚ vs gadir, a grete lord*e* es he,
W*ith* our flesche *and* our felle als we i*n* werlde were,
And neuere saƚƚ sonderyn*g* fra þat day be
  To knawe.
Oure werkes are wretyn [*and*] scorde,
In a role of recorde,   414
Be-fore þat ilk grete lorde
  Fuƚƚ scharply to schawe.

XXXIII

WE saƚƚ seke thedyr i*n* sympiƚƚ atyre,
  Tremland *and* qwakande als lefe appon tree,
When aƚƚ [is] vmbsett wi*th* wat*er and* †fyre,
Þer may no wrenke ne no wyle wysse vs to flye,   420
When cryst es greued so sare he es a grym syre,
So many a synfuƚƚ wreche als [h]e saƚƚ þer see ;
Þan dare noghte his modir, þofe scho wold gyff hyre,
Speke tiƚƚ hir dere sone, so dredfuƚƚ es hee,

399 B ne kyn. 402 A onane : B alane. 404 count] B courte. 405 soyttures] B þ*er* seyn. 406-7 These lines, being in MS. A the bottom line of f. 100 v, are mutilated, and only the top halves of the letters remain in most cases : B The saule *and* þe body þat lang has ben sere Be-ho*u*es to be sam at þat sembelee. 408 at fett] B to seche. 413 A in : B *and*. 418 qwakande] B schakand*e*. 419 A aƚƚ vmbsett wi*th* wat*er and* wi*th* fyre : B al is vmbesett wi*th* wi*th* wat*er and* fire. 422 B So many synfuƚƚ wreches as. A we : B he. 423 B yf scho wald*e* desyre.

An Alliterative Religious Lyric

Þat day.
Alle þe halowes of heueñ
Saƚƚ be stiƚƚ of þaire steueñ,
Dare þay noghte a worde neueñ,
Fo[r] na mañ to praye.

XXXIV

PAÑ þe werkes of mercy he rekenysse alle seueñ:
'Wheñ þat I was hungry how haue ȝe me fe[dde]?
When I askede ȝow a drynk ȝe ne harde not my steueñ,
And wheñ I was naked how haue ȝe me cled[de]?
Or wheñ I was howseles horberd ȝe me [eueñ],
Or vesett me in sekenesse or soghte to my bedde,
Or comforthede me in preson, þat wolde [I] here neue[ñ],
Or broghte me to beryi*n*g wheñ dede me by-stedd[e]?'
Þay say:
'Lorde, wheñ sawe we the,
†Euer in swylk a degree?'
'Þe leste in the name of me,
Þat to ȝow myghte pray.'

XXXV

HE schaƚƚ schew his wondis blody *and* bare,
Als he hase sofferde for oure sake, wytt*er and* wyde;
Kynges *and* kaysers by-fore hy*m* þañ saƚƚ fare,
Byschopis *and* baroun*es and* aƚƚ bus habyde,
Erelles *and* Emp*er*ours † nane wiƚƚ he spare,
Prestys *and* p*er*sones *and* prelatis of pryde,
Thies Iustyce *and* mellarse of lawe *and* of lare,
Þat now are fuƚƚ ryalle to ryne *and* to ryde
In lande,
Þaire dome saƚƚ þay take þare,
Ryghte als þay demyd are,
Wheñ þay ware of myghtis mare,
And domes hadde i*n* hande.

426

432

438

444

450

---

428 A *neuenn* altered to *neueñ*: B neueñ.   429 A Fo: B For.   431 hungry] MS. A has an extra stroke in the *n*.   fedde] B fed*e*.   433 B cled*e*.
434 A neu*er*: B eueñ.   436 A ȝe here neu*er*: B I her*e* neueñ.   437 B had me sted*e*.   440 A Eueu*er* (? = Eu*er*, with *eu* repeated).   444 B bytt*er*.
445 B before hy*m* bus fare.   447 A for nane: B nane.   449 B Þar just*es* and þ*er* domes m*en* of lawe or of lar*e*.

XXXVI

THIRE ladyse are arayede in robys ful ȝare,　　456
Revers *and* rebanes w*ith* gownne *and* w*ith* gyde,
Bendys and botonys, felettis *and* fare,
Golde one þaire garlandis, perry *and* pryde,
Kelles *and* corchyfes at cou*er*e þaire hare,
So schaply *and* schynand to schewe by þair hyde;
Alle þat welthe es a-way *and* myrthe mekiłł mare,　　462
Bot if we wyn þat trewlufe vnglade † may we glyde,
　　For sorowe.
　Be-tyme es beste þat we blyn̄,
　　If we be fune fułł of syn̄,
　Þer es no kythe ne no kyn̄
　　Fra bale may vs borowe.　　468

XXXVII

BE lordis *and* be ladys not alle tełł I,
Bot alswa by oþ*er* I fynde fułł fele:
Thies galiarde gedlynges þat kythes gentry,
W*ith* denyvs damysels þ*er* many men̄ dele,
With p*ur*fełłe *and* peloure *and* hedys fułł hye;
Hir corse es i*n* mydwarde [of] hir catele,　　474
If men carpe of hir kyn̄ a-waye wiłł scho wry,　[f. 101 v.]
Hir fadir *and* hir modir fayne wolde scho hele
　　And hyde.
　Bot when þat day sałł begyn̄,
　　Þan schames nane w*ith* þair kyn̄,
　Bot ałł may þam schame w*ith* þair syn,　　480
　　And w*ith* þair fułł pryde.

XXXVIII

ÞE dome of þat trewlufe ful sare may we drede,
For þan es tyme paste of m*er*cy to craue,
When Ilk man̄ sałł be demede aft*er* his awenn dede;
Þan may we not ourselfe sytt *and* sende forthe our knau[e],

---

457 A *gown*n̄ altered to *gownn*e　　458 botonys] B meroures.　　459-61 B Golde on̄ þ*er* garland*es* perly *and* p*r*ide Kell*es and* kerchyff*es* cowchede ou*er* þ*er* hare So schaply *and* semand*e* to schew by þ*er* syde.　　463 A vngladly: B vnglad*e*.　　466 A *fun̄* apparently changed to *fune* in the MS.: B fon̄.　469 alle] B anely.　　471-2 B þis kaliard*e* godlyn͠g kythes gentrye W*ith* dengyouse damesels þ*er* may men dele.　　474 of] A in: B of.　　481 B foule.　　485 B þan̄ may not owr*e* self stert *and* send furth our*e* knafe.

An Alliterative Religious Lyric

He rekkenys by resoune als ☦ clerkes rede, 486
He settis one his ryght hande þat he will saue,
Thase wafull wyghtis, þat may not per spede,
[Sal stande on] his left-hande] and ☦ wa sall þay haue
    For ay.
Þan will our lady wepe sare,
For sorow þat scho sees þare, 492
When scho may helpe no mare,
    Grete dole es þat day.

XXXIX

BOT now es tyme for to speke who-so will spede,
And for to seke socoure and folys ☦ to fle,
And noghte appon domesdaye when we haue maste nede;
For nowe es mekill mercy and þan sall nane be, 498
When oure lady Marie dare nott for drede
Speke till hir dere son, so dredfull es he.
How may þay hafe mercy for þaire mysdede,
Þat will not folowe þer-to, when þat it es fre
    And [ȝ]are?
Ther es no way bot twa, 504
Vn-to wele or to wa,
Whethir-so sall [we] ga,
    We duell euer-mare.'

XL

THUS this trewe turtyll techis this may,
Scho blyssede his body, his bone and his blode.
Vn-to þat ilke ferthe lefe I rede þat we praye, 510
Þat scho will bere oure message with a mylde mode,
And þat scho speke for oure lufe bi-fore þat laste day,
Vn-to þase ilke iij leues þat we may wyn with mode;
Þat grace grauntede grete gode þat dyede on gud fryday,
Vn-to þat ilke ferthe lefe gracyouse and gude,

486 A als thies clerkes rede: B als clarkes rede. 487 B haue. 489
Sal ... wa] so B : A þair sange es of sorowe and swa. 496 A folys for to
fle: B folys to flee. 503 A thare : B ȝare. 506 A Whethir so sall to
ga: B Wheder þat we schall ga. 508 B teches hys may. 512 oure etc.] B þat
ilk lufe. 513-15 leues etc.] B lefes gracyous and gude þe lufe of þase iiii lefes at
we wyn may þat grace grante gret god þat diede on a rode.

>   Þat kynge. 516
> This herde I in a lay,
> Als I wente one my way,
> In a mornynge of may,
>   Wheñ medowes sall sprynge.

517 lay] B walay.

NOTES

l. 1. *salł*, i.e. 'do necessarily'. For the various uses of *shall* denoting necessity, fate, obligation, see *sculan* in Bosworth Toller.

spryng is here used transitively to mean 'produce, bring forth', with *blomes and blossomes* in l. 2 as its object. The earliest transitive use in this sense given in *O.E.D.* is dated 1525, though it is so used figuratively in *The Paston Letters*, iii. 130 (1475).

3. *welle*, i.e. a spring of water rising to the surface of the earth and forming a small pool or flowing in a stream, a pool fed by a spring; cp. Holy Well and the various saints' wells. A flower-bedecked garden with a well is a conventional medieval literary setting; see the description of the wells in the garden of the *Romaunt of the Rose*, A, ll. 1409-38. In *Floriz and Blauncheflur* (ed. McKnight, p. 90) the well in the garden has streams which come from Paradise. See also *The Visions of Tundale* (ed. Turnbull, pp. 49-50), and the hymn *Verbum Caro Factum Est* (*The Visions of Tundale*, ed. Turnbull, p. 157) which describes a scene very much like the one in this poem:

> 'I passud thorow a garden grene
> I fond a herbere made full newe
> A semelyor syght I haff noght sene
> O ylke tree sange a tyrtull trew
> Theryn a maydon bryght off hew
> And ever sche sange,' &c.

on my playing, i.e. 'in my diversion' or 'in my exercise', the second interpretation being perhaps more suitable here; cp. *Pis. of Sus.* (st. XVII), where the priests say: 'we passed us to play, Of preiere and of penaunce was vre purpose.'

4. *a mery orcherde*, i.e. 'a pleasant garden'. For *mery* in the now obsolete sense of 'pleasant in aspect or conditions,'—its original meaning in the expression 'Merry England'—cp. Trevisa (*Barth. de P. R.* XV. v) on Armenia: 'It is moste meri londe with herbes, corne, wodes, and fruite'.

bedande myn̄ hourres, i.e. 'saying my Office', *bedande* having the meaning of OE. *biddan*, 'to pray', but taking its form from OE. *bēodan*, 'to offer'. The *hourres* were the seven Canonical Hours, or (as here) those portions of the Divine office appointed to be recited at those hours, viz. Matins with Lauds, Prime, Tierce, Sext, None, Vespers, and Compline.

6. *belde to þᵉ boures*, i.e. 'raise or construct gradually the bowers, i.e. the glades, coverts, arbours. ME. *belden*, 'to build', < OE. * *byldan*, has two fundamental senses, (1) to construct a dwelling, (2) to dwell. For the latter meaning see ll. 147 and 316 with note. It is here used figuratively in the sense of 'construct, raise, frame by gradual means anything compared to an edifice'. For its use with *to* and *toward* in this sense cp. *Gesta Rom.* (E.E.T.S. p. 86) MS. Harl.: 'All þat is ayens conscience, beldith toward helle', where Add. MS. reads: 'edefieth Helle',

and 1526 *Pilgr. Perf.* (*W. de W.* 1531), 36: 'That . . . they may meryte & buylde to theyr crowne in heuen '. The use here of *boures* in the sense of 'glades, coverts, arbours', is a very early one. B reads: ' belde to þare bores '.

8. *sekande*, i.e. 'sickening' with the sense of 'pining with yearning ', from ME. *sēken*, ' to be sick', < the adj. *sēoc*, ' sick'. Cp. Hawes's *Pas. of Pl.* xvi. (*E.E.T.S.* l. 1599): ' My hert sekened and began waxe sore'.

11. *me*, added to the text from MS. B to improve both sense and metre.

16. *kertchefs . . . ketle.* See Note to l. 460.

17. *hir*, an addition from B to improve both sense and metre.

19. *i-wys*, added from B for metrical reasons.

noghte. This word is supplied from B as folio 98 of MS. A is damaged at the edge, so that some words and parts of words at the ends of lines in the recto are missing. With the help of MS. B these have been restored to the text, and enclosed in square brackets. See also ll. 6, 17, 28, 30, 43, 47.

20. *be I dede*, i.e. 'may I be dead '.

23. *turtilt*, i.e. ' turtle-dove '. The turtle-dove is often mentioned as a type of conjugal affection and constancy because, as a ME. Bestiary says, she keeps to one mate and never leaves him ; if he dies she never takes another but keeps her old love in her heart as if he were still alive. In this, she is an emblem of the soul which should ever be true to Christ, her spiritual mate. See *A Bestiary* (*OE. Miscellany*, ed. Morris).

31–2. *duelle to comforthe*, i.e. ' delay to comfort ', the infinitive *to comforthe* being the object of *duelle*. For the transitive use of *duelle* see Orm. (l. 13218): '[He] ne dwalde nohht to kiþenn himm '.

33. *with buke and with belle*, i.e. the missal and the sanctuary bell used in the service of the Mass. This was a frequent asseveration in the Middle Ages, and was used in a form of excommunication. Cp. *Cursor Mundi*, vol. iii, l. 25038, : ' cursed he is wiþ boke & belle '.

39. *scho*, i.e. Our Lady, of l. 37. In A *scho* is corrected to *he* in a later hand ; this would refer the blessing to ' company' of l. 38, i.e. the turtle-dove. The earlier reading seems more appropriate here.

42. *trewe-lufe*, i.e. the four-leaved clover or quatrefoil of love, the whorl of four leaves with the single flower or berry in the midst suggesting the figure of the true-love knot. It also means ' a faithful lover, a true-love '. The word is used indiscriminately in both senses, viz. the quatrefoil and the lover, throughout this poem, though we find *trewlufe grysse*, 'true-love grass', in l. 66 for the plant. The scribe of MS. B seems to have confused the adjective *trewful(l)*, ' faithful ' with *trewful(l)* = (?) *trefoil*, 'three-leaved clover'. (See B readings to ll. 42, 319, 326, 339). The old rhyme illustrates the association of the quatrefoil with a lover:

> 'If you find an even ash-leaf,
> Or a four-leaved clover,
> You'll be bound to see your true-love
> Ere the day be over.'

The four-leaved clover as the symbol of true love and applied by the poet to the Trinity and the Virgin Mary suggested to Gollancz the title for this poem. For another example of the exaltation of Mary until she is regarded almost as a fourth person of the Trinity, cp. the practice among Sicilian peasants of signing their tools with four parallel strokes to signify the Father, Son, and Holy Ghost, and the most Holy Mary (Th. Trede, quoted by Coulton in *Five Centuries of Religion*, i. 139).

55. *Alle thi sythe may þou sighe*, i.e. 'All thy life-time may thou sigh'; ME. *sithe, sythe*, 'journey, course of one's life' < OE. *sīþ*. After *may* we expect *haue* instead of *hade* in l. 56, but as both MSS. have the past tense, it is better to keep it in the text. It was probably used to agree with the past *knewe*, which was needed for the rhyme, as the sense does not require the past subjunctive expressing improbability.

mare. I take this as the adverb modifying the positive *nere* and so forming the comparative 'nearer'.

56. *concette*, i.e. 'secret, confidential knowledge'.

57. *spryngande* [*and*] *euer-more newe*, i.e. 'growing and eternally fresh.' This B reading is somewhat better than the A text without *and*.

60. *sett for to seke ȝit*, i.e. 'set on still seeking', *ȝit* implying continuance from the past up to and at the present time, i.e. = 'still'.

63. *luf*, 'love', from B, obviously a better reading than *lyf(e)* of A. MS. A is here torn and repaired and faint traces of what may be *e* appear after *lyf*.

67. *lefes*, 'leaves', omitted in A, probably through a scribal oversight.

70. *heuen-paradise.* This is not merely repetitive, for *heuen* = the heavens generally, the firmament, whereas by *paradise* is denoted the heavenly paradise, the abode of God and his angels. The Jews recognized seven heavens, the highest, called also 'heaven of heavens', being the abode of God and the most exalted angels. Cp. 'the third heaven' (2 Cor. xii. 2) and 'the heaven and heaven of heavens' (1 Kings viii. 27).

71. *þis merie medilerthe*, i.e. 'this pleasant earth'. For *merie* in this sense see note to l. 4. The form *medilerthe* is described in *O.E.D.* as an etymologizing perversion of *middle-erd* < OE. *middanȝeard* = the world, the earth as situated between heaven and hell, *-ȝeard* becoming later *-eard* by association with *eard*, 'a dwelling', and *middel-* being substituted for *middan-*. For this conception of the position of the earth between heaven and hell, see also Milton, *Par. Lost*, ii. 1047:

> 'Far off the empyreal Heaven, extended wide
> In circuit, undetermined square or round . . .
> And, fast by, hanging in a golden chain,
> This pendent World.'

73. *vs awe*, 'it behoves us', with quasi-impersonal use of the verb and dative, the subject being the infinitives which follow.

75. *ȝour*. There is no need to adopt the B reading *þⁱ* instead of the plural *ȝour*, for the author here suddenly ceases to speak in the person of the turtle-dove to the girl and is now, in his double role of cleric and author, addressing a wider audience, viz. all the readers of his poem.

76. The omission of *may*, as in B, improves both sense and metre.

77. *kynde*, i.e. 'kind, family, race'. The word does not pair very well with *trewlufe*, but the poet needed a rhyme with *mynde* and *fynde*, hence *kynde*.

79. *bi - - soñ*, i.e. 'I represent or symbolize God's son by this same second leaf'.

80. *es*, i.e. 'he is', or 'who is', the subject being included in the verb.

81. *to-gedir þay wone*, i.e. 'they abide together'. This is the reading of B; A gives *to-gedir are done*, which makes little sense. For the use of the clover as an apt illustration of the doctrine of the Trinity, three persons yet only one God, cp. the legend of St. Patrick and the shamrock. Medieval art made use of various devices to depict this Trinity in Unity, finest and best-known of all perhaps being the representation, as in Dürer's Adoration of the Trinity, of the crucified Christ between the knees of the Father, with the Dove hovering over both. In the case of the quatrefoil the Virgin Mary is included (see note to l. 42).

84. *comly, &c.* This line refers to 'kynge' in l. 83 and means 'comely of hue or countenance, gracious and fair'.

85. *hym one*, i.e. 'him only', almost meaning 'himself'. See *O.E.D.* for *one*, 'alone', almost meaning 'self' after pronouns.

87. *off grace*, i.e. 'of or by grace'.

89. MS. B omits the repetition of 'with' before 'water', and as this is metrically better, B reading has been adopted here.

91. *face*, i.e. 'semblance, appearance, outward form'; cp. *P. Pl. Crede* (E.E.T.S. l. 670): 'þei schulden nouȝt after þe face neuer þe folke demen'. See note to l. 114.

93. *paradisse*, i.e. the carthly paradise, the garden of Eden.

96. *Sathanasse*, i.e. 'Satan'. According to *O.E.D.* those forms of the name which in ME. ended in *-as, -ase, -ace* came from the emphatic Jewish Aramaic form, through Greek, Vulgate Latin (Satanās), and in some cases Old French, into Middle English. The form Satān, from the unemphatic Hebrew form, is found in the Vulgate only in the Old Testament.

97. *þer*, when used emphatically means 'in that respect'; cp. Shak. *Rom. and Jul.* III. iii. 137, 'thy Juliet is alive ... There art thou happy'. It is commonly used in ME. to introduce an imprecation, and with practically no meaning, as here. Cp. *Cant. T.* (B 602): 'ther God yeve him meschance!'

102. *hym froo*, i.e. 'from him', the preposition following its object.

104. *a nappiłł*, i.e. 'an apple', an example of the transference of *-n* from the indefinite article to a noun beginning with a vowel. Cp. *newt* and *nickname*.

108. *hym bi-forne*, 'before him', the preposition following its object.

109–10. These lines mean: 'Thou shalt go to Maid Mary [as] my messenger and [shalt] bear her joyous tidings [that] I will to be born of her'.

111. *sone*. For angels described as sons of God, see Job i. 6.

114. *face* seems here to mean 'person', but *O.E.D.* gives no authority for that meaning, though *face* is used in the sense of 'outward form, semblance', as in l. 91. It also has some reference to beauty in the expressions 'full of face' (*O.E.D.* 1608) and 'to be in face' (*O.E.D.* 1773). Possibly in this context we have an example of metonymy, the face as the most obvious part of the person standing for the whole person; or perhaps we should read *faire of face* in the text.

121. *mett*, i.e. 'had carnal knowledge of'. The doctrine of the Virgin Birth is here alluded to.

122–3. These two lines mean: 'Look at your cousin; Elizabeth, who has long been prevented, has this year in her old age conceived'. For *beholde to* in the sense of 'look at', cp. Wyclif, Gen. iv. 4: 'the Lord bihelde to Abel and to his ȝiftis'.

[*e*]*lde*, i.e. 'old age', B reads *held*. Folio 98 of MS. A has been torn and repaired, but in a good light *elde* is discernible, the initial *e* alone being rather doubtful. The word is from OE. *eldo, yldo*, and corresponds to the Wyclifite *elde, eelde*, in the same context. Compare the Vulgate: 'in senectute sua'.

lett, i.e. 'prevented'; the word is supplied from MS. B as A is torn in the corner.

131. *owr*. Sense and metre are improved by the adoption of this word from B.

132. *þat lady*. A reads *a maydeñ* which is repeated in l. 134. B reading has been adopted to avoid this repetition and for the sake of alliteration.

133. This line refers to 'þat lady' in the previous line.

137. *choseñ for chaste*, i.e. 'chosen for, on account of, chastity', the adjective *chaste* being here used substantively; cp. 'for slepeles' in *Parl. of Thre Ages* (Roxburghe Club, 1897), p. 49, where Gollancz notes the not uncommon occurrence of this idiomatic adjectival formation in ME. alliterative poetry.

140. *foure*. The scribe of A first wrote *thre*, which he corrected to *foure*.

144. A reads: 'Now all thies foure louely leues a frende to þam̄ hase tane', whereas B has: 'Now has þer iij leues a fourte fela tañ'. The scribe of A was apparently confused by having to go back in his story and resume from l. 136.

147. *bryghte*, i.e. 'a beautiful woman'; cp. Henry, *Wallace*, v. 612: 'throuch bewté off that brycht'.

150. *schynede and schane*. The strong and weak predicates of the same verb, ME. *schinen* < OE. *scīnan*, are here used in a metrical tag. B reads 'schewed' instead of 'schynede'.

157. *þis*, i.e. 'these', a ME. plural form agreeing with *tythynges*, a plural noun. B reads *þase tythandes*, 'those tidings'.

158. *knaw*, i.e. 'male', has been added to the text from B.

159. *Garte he make*, i.e. 'he caused to be made'.

160. *knaue childer*, i.e. 'male children'. This is the reading of B, a better one than 'þat knaue childe' of A, as Matt. ii. 16 seems to be alluded to rather than Matt. ii. 8.

161. *in qwarte*, i.e. 'alive and well', the noun *qwarte* meaning 'health, the state of being alive and well'. The phrase here seems to mean no more than 'alive'.

173. *Baptiste*, i.e. 'baptised'. The scribe of A seems to use the name 'Baptist' as the verb; B more distinctly uses the word as a verb: *hym baptyste*. This form of the preterite is not in *O.E.D.*

175. *hafe slane*. These words are supplied from B, as folio 99 of MS. A is damaged at the edge so that words and parts of words are missing at the ends of lines. These have been restored after collation with B and enclosed in square brackets. See also ll. 145, 149, 151, 171, 177, 186, 188, 190, 191, 197, 199.

fele famen, i.e. 'fell or cruel foemen'. I take *fele* in this sense rather than as meaning 'many', as 'foemen fell' is such a stock phrase.

185. *leue lordynges*, i.e. ' dear Sirs '; *lordynges*, either with or without the adjective, was often used in ME. address; cp. the beginning of Chaucer's *Somn. T.* and elsewhere.

186. *say*. I take this as the infinitive, i.e. 'whatever you would say'; cp. *Siege of Jer.* (*E.E.T.S.*) l. 544, 'hente who so wolde'.

194. *ȝare*. A reading *þare*, a repetition of the rhyming word in l. 192, is obviously a mistake, probably for *yare = ȝare*, as the MS. confuses *y* and *þ*. B, which also confuses *þ* and *y*, reads *yare*, probably for *ȝare*. See also lines 375 and 503.

196. *was*. This may be another instance of the inclusion of the subject in the verb, *was* meaning 'who was'; cp. ll. 221, 222, 223. The earliest instance of the use of *alas for* given in *O.E.D.* is Milton's *Par. Lost*, xi. 461: 'Alas, both for the deed and for the cause!' Or we may suppose a comma after *alas*, and take *for* as a conjunction and *lefe* as the subject of *was*.

197. *felauchip*, i.e., 'companion'. *O.E.D.* gives only the abstract and collective uses of the word.

204. *with gatte*. The choice lay between the meaningless tag: *with*

atte, of A and the repetition of 'gall' as in B, when it has already occurred in a different form, *attir*, in l. 203.

214. *ryue*. i.e. 'rend, split', used transitively with 'temple' as its object.

222. *þan*. So A; B reads *ȝitt*, but there is little to choose between the readings. The narrator is going back in his story (as he did in l. 144) and taking it up again from l. 200.

223. *was*, i.e. 'who was'; for the omission of the relative pronoun cp. ll. 221, 222.

225. *to þⁱ soñ*, i.e. 'for thy son'. Cp. the expression 'take to wife'.

226. In both MSS. this line is corrupt. The reading of A: *take mary þⁱ moder now to þᵉ*, is obscure in meaning and faulty metrically; that of B: *take mary to þⁱ moder mary to þᵉ*, makes no sense. Gollancz proposed changing *þⁱ* to *mⁱ* and adding *moder* in the second half of the line. This makes good sense and translates thus: 'take my mother Mary now as thy mother'.

228. *Longeus*, i.e. Longinus of medieval legend. The story of the blind Longinus piercing the side of the crucified Christ with a spear and recovering his sight through the blood that fell on his eyes owes, if not its origin, certainly much of its popularity to the apocryphal Gospel of Nicodemus, and is based on John xix. 34. Longinus and the Bloody Spear was a favourite subject in medieval art (e.g. Ferrari's fresco on the Crucifixion at Varallo) and drama, and the story had an important influence on the development of the Holy Grail story in Arthurian legend. See preface to W. H. Hulme's edition of the ME. *Harrowing of Hell* and *Gospel of Nicodemus*. See also the account of the incident in *Cursor Mundi*, ed. Morris, vol. ii, pp. 963-4.

239. *myghtis*, i.e. 'power'. In OE. the noun was often used in the plural with singular meaning, e.g. *eallum hire mihtum and mægenum*, 'with all her might and main' (Lchdm. II, 352, l. 5), and for a later Scotch instance see *The Merry Wives of Musleburgh, etc.*, st. 31: 'I wan aff be Mights of Marie' (Pennecuik, *Comp. Coll. Poems*, 1750?).

249. *sight*. A reads *light*, obviously in error; B gives *syght*.

250. *hope*, i.e. 'anticipate', without any sense of desire; cp. R. of Brunne, *Handl. Synne*, ll. 6966-7 (1303): 'he yn þe feuer lay, And to þe deþe he hoped weyl'. B reads *trow*.

251. *fare*, i.e. 'commotion', a derivative meaning of ME. *fare* < OE. *faru*, 'a going', hence 'mode of proceeding', hence 'display, commotion, fuss'.

253. *thare the nogte layne* literally means: 'there is need for thee to conceal nothing', i.e., as in B, 'thou must conceal nothing'. But *thare* really = 'dare' here. (See *O.E.D.* for confusion of forms of *dare* and *thar*.) Here too the impersonal construction plus dative seems to have been borrowed from *thar*, as this seems to be the only example of *dare* used impersonally.

255. *pitt*, i.e. 'pit of hell,' hell or some part of it being conceived as a sunken place, or as a dungeon or place of confinement; cp. *York Mys.* xxxvii. 348: 'I synke in to helle pitte'. Hell, in the sense of hades, was conceived as the abode of all departed spirits, good and bad. These latter, judging by the reference, here and elsewhere, to pain, were apparently suffering. *Limbo patrum* was a region supposed to exist on the border of hell, and here the souls of the just who had died before Christ awaited his coming, without suffering the pains of hell; cp. 1526 *Pilgr. Perf.* (W. de W. 1531) 53 b, 'After theyr deth they went to lymbo patrum a place of derknes nye to hell'.

261. *heried he helle*, i.e. 'he despoiled hell of its captives', the souls of the just who could not enter heaven until Christ had redeemed them. He took away the just and left the wicked behind; cp. *St. Erkenwald*, l. 292, where the soul of the pagan judge was left behind. The descent into hell was formally recognized as part of the Christian faith in the fourth century, when it was introduced into the Apostles' Creed, though there was controversy as to the purpose of the descent. From the tenth century onward the harrowing of hell appears constantly in Christian literature and art (see Fra Angelico, Ferrari, Dürer, etc.), and it is a constant theme in ME. literature; see the ME. poem of the name, the account in *Cursor Mundi* (ed. Morris, vol. ii, p. 1031), etc. and note Chaucer, *Mill. T.* 326: 'By him that harwed helle'.

263. *Dauyd, his derlynge*, i.e. 'David, his well beloved', a phrase based on 1 Sam. xiii. 14, where David is described as 'a man after his [*sc.* the Lord's] own heart'.

265. This line I take as referring to Christ rather than to David; l. 266 certainly refers to Christ.

267. *fette*, i.e. 'dire, grievous'. It might possibly be taken as a variant of *fele*, 'many', as the form *fett(e)*, 'many', occurs from the fourteenth to sixteenth centuries, but the B reading *snett*, 'grievous, painful', supports the other interpretation.

268, *bon*, i.e. 'good'; the French word was adopted into ME. from OF. MS. B reads *gud*.

270. *noghte for to layne*, i.e. 'not to be concealed'.

273. *haly gaste*. The reference is not to the Holy Ghost, the third person of the Trinity, but to the soul of Christ which had been down to hell and now returned to the body to raise it to life.

284. For the Scriptural authority for this episode see Mark xvi. 9.

287-93. Our author varies the Gospel story in which Mary Magdalene tells of Christ's Resurrection to all the disciples who 'believed not' (Mark xvi. 11). Thomas, according to John xx. 25, refused to believe the other apostles. The poet probably had Luke xxiv. 10-11 in mind, and made Thomas spokesman for the rest of the Apostles.

Thomas of ynde, i.e. St. Thomas the Apostle who, after preaching the

Notes

Gospel in Parthia and the East generally, is said to have suffered martyrdom at Meliapor, on the coast of Coromandel, where his body was discovered with certain marks which pointed to his having been slain with lances. In 1523 his relics were found by the Portuguese in a chapel vault outside Meliapor, and a new town of St. Thomas rose about this church. St. Thomas's feast is kept by the Latins on December 21st and by the Indians on July 1st.

292. *carpand*, 'chattering, prating', the participial adjective. So in B ; A less satisfactorily reads *of carpynge*.

293-4. The meaning of these lines is : 'He [Thomas] would never believe that Christ himself went about, ere he [Christ] appeared', etc. B reads *or* for *þat* in l. 293, and omits *Or he* in l. 294, so meaning : 'He [Thomas] would never believe it ere Christ himself went [and] appeared', etc.

300. *a sothe for to say*. This is just a metrical tag ; B reads *þ*ᵉ for *a*, and so gives the sense that Christ went forth to declare the truth, which idea is repeated in the second half of l. 301.

302. *þat lady*, i.e. Christ's Mother.

303. *alle hale of his hurtes*, i.e. 'quite healed of his injuries'. The doctrine of the Glorified Body was expanded by the Schoolmen from the 'spiritual body' of 1 Cor. xv. 44, and the bodies of the just after resurrection were endowed by them with four gifts, viz. impassibility ; splendour, the glory of the soul shining forth in the body ; subtlety, the power of penetrating other bodies ; agility, the power of moving and acting swiftly at the will of the spirit.

306. *one halowe thoresday*, i.e. on Ascension Thursday. The epithet 'holy' was applied to various Thursdays, e.g. Rogation Thursday, Maundy Thursday, and Corpus Christi Day. I take *one* as the preposition meaning 'on', that being likelier than the sense 'one.' B reads *oñ*.

307. *his moder*. The doctrine of the Assumption and Coronation of Our Lady in Heaven figured much in medieval art (e.g. Botticelli, Titian, Correggio, etc.) and literature (e.g. *The Golden Legend, Assumption of Our Lady*, and the ME. poems, *Assumpcio beate Marie* (ed. McKnight, *E.E.T.S.*), *Cursor Mundi* (vol. iii, p. 1146, etc.).

314. *child*. Folio 100 of MS. A is damaged at the edge, so that some words and parts of words are missing. After reference to MS. B these have been supplied and enclosed in square brackets. See also ll. 288, 294, 301, 305, 307, 316, 318, 327, 331, 333.

316. *vn-to þam bathe belde*, i.e. 'abide with them both', *belde* being supplied from B. The scribe of A first wrote *gl*, as if about to write *glide*, but this he erased, and *b* with traces of *e* following it appear below (see previous note). For *belde* used intransitively in the sense of 'dwell', cp. 'The holy goste will in the byldon' (Turnbull : *The Visions of Tundale*, p. 142), and see note to l. 6. For *unto* supplying the place of the dative,

see *Alph. of Tales* (E.E.T.S.) pt. I, p. 207 : 'He putt þaim [sc. his goods] vnto þe bisshopp'; though it may be our scribe wrote *vn-to* with the verb *glide* in his mind.

317. *a*, i.e. 'one'; the definite numeral, the apocopate form of *an*, *ane* (< OE. *ān*, 'one'), used only before a consonant from the twelfth century onward.

319. *tre*, i.e. 'plant', or perhaps 'stem'. This word originally meaning 'tree' was, according to *O.E.D.*, extended to include bushes and shrubs of erect growth and having a single stem, e.g. 'rose-tree'. In *E.D.D.* we find *tre* used to denote 'a plant grown in a pot; a small bush-like shrub', and as an example of the former use an Edgmond child is quoted as saying, on seeing a gardener bedding-out geraniums: "'e's plontin' treys'. The word might be applied to the clover on account of its form.

trewlufe, i.e. 'quatrefoil'. B, both here and in l. 326, reads *trewfull* = (?) 'trefoil'. See note to l. 42.

321. *So hende*, i.e. 'so gracious'; a metrical tag.

324. *þer*, i.e. 'where', the relative adverb. B reads *whar*.

331. *As fercost in flode*, i.e. 'as ship in the deep'. The word *fercost*, <ON. *farkostr*, means an 'inferior kind of boat or ship'. Skene mentions a late fifteenth-century reference to 'ane Fercost, quhilk is inferior in birth and quantity to ane Schip' (*De Verb. Sign.*).

332. *in bonddage ... be*, i.e. 'under obligation to be in bale'; *bonddage* here meaning 'binding force, obligation'.

333. *hert blode*, i.e. 'heart's blood', *hert* being a survival of the OE. weak feminine genitive ending in *-an*, ME. *-e*, which was later lost. B writes *awñ blode*.

339. *trewlufe*, i.e. 'quatrefoil'. B reads *trewfull* with *full* erased and *luf* written above the erasure. See note to l. 42.

340. *at assaye*, i.e. 'to try, to test'; *assaye* is more likely to be the infinitive than the noun, though B reads *in faye* after the adjectives.

341. *þer*, i.e. 'these', *þer* being the Scotch and Northern form of the demonstrative adjective; cp. *thire* in l. 456.

342-7. This conception of the Virgin Mary as Mediator between us and an outraged Christ was general in medieval times and had largely replaced the Pauline doctrine of Christ as our mediator with God the Father. The change was due partly to the medieval association of Christ, as here, with the severity of the Last Judgement, and partly to feudal conceptions of the influence of 'the queen'. If the obvious meaning of l. 423 is allowed, then Mary is in this poem represented as willing to buy her Son's mercy for us with a gift. For the idea of Mary as Queen and Mediator, cp. *Pearl*, st. 37:

'That emperise al heuenȝ hatȝ,
And vrthe and helle in her bayly.'

See also the *Song to the Virgin* (*OE. Misc.*, ed. Morris, p. 195), *The*

Golden Legend (Temple Cl. iv. 251) where Mary weighs down the balance of her client's good deeds and so saves him at the judgement, *Soul's Ward*, and *A Good Orison of Our Lady* (*OE. Homilies*, ed. Morris), in which poem Mary is represented as making her friends all rich kings, giving them royal robes, bracelets and gold rings. In our poem, however, Mary is not so much the queen as the gentle petitioner. See ll. 499–500 and note.

344. *eghne graye*, 'grey eyes', a desirable feature in the Middle Ages, if we can judge from contemporary complimentary references; cp. Wright, *Lyric Poems*, p. 39, 'that swete thyng with eȝenen gray', and Chaucer, *Reeve's T.* 54 :
'This wenche thikke and wel y-growen was,
With camuse nose and eyen greye as glas.'
Malone in his gloss on Shakespeare (*Works*, 1821, vol. iv, p. 118) writes: 'By a *grey* eye was meant, what we now call a *blue* eye.'

352. *dewe*, i.e. 'proper, true'; cp. 'þe dewe dame' (Langl. *Rich. Redeles*, III, 60). B reads *derñ*, 'privy, crafty'.

356–7. The meaning is : 'It pleases us never to believe it, [either] for priest or for friar, Ere we feel that we fall (i.e. die) we faint and we swoon', the idea apparently being that before we realize that we are dying (we refused to believe the priest or friar when he told us), we fall into unconsciousness. B reads *with swelt or with swone*, i.e. we fall 'with fainting (?) or with swooning', and connects *or* with *leue*, giving the meaning of our refusal to believe in death before we experience it. *O.E.D.* does not give *swelt* as a noun.

366. *And we be*, i.e. 'if we be', *and* being the conditional conjunction meaning 'if'. The sense of this and the preceding line is that it does not matter about the body if we can be sure where our soul will go. The scribe of B, to denote the impossibility of our ever being sure, put the line into the past tense : *And we ware sykere of owr sales ware we schulde dwell.*

369. *felle*, i.e. 'grievous, hard', the meaning of the whole phrase being : 'what hard ways nor how far'. The B reading *How fell ne how fayr* reproduces the contrast of the Bible and, in its use of the singular in l. 370, *harde way is*, B is also closer to the text of Matt. vii. 13–14.

vs falles, literally = 'it befalls, happens to us'; here it means : 'it is allotted to us, it is fated us'.

379. *glasyng*, i.e. 'slipping, gliding', from OF. *glacer*, 'to glide, slip'. The B reading *gladynge* is given in *O.E.D.* only in the sense of 'rejoicing'.

381. *euerylke a*, i.e. 'every'. The use of the adjective with *a* or *an* before the substantive is common in Middle English. Compare *ilk a*, which from the fifteenth century is generally written *ilka*.

383. *frayste of þat fare*, i.e. 'asked of that multitude'; *frayste* < ON. *freista*, means 'try, experience, or ask'. In the only example of its use with *of* given in *O.E.D.*, it means 'ask', viz. *Destr. of Troy* (E.E.T.S.), l. 97 : 'ffrayne will I fer and fraist of þere werkes'.

384. *of* is Gollancz's emendation. A reads *es* and B *is*. Though the emendation improves the text, sense could be made of the A reading, viz. 'But all our sorrow is then, no certain end [*sc.* of it] we know'; but B which also omits *ende* makes no sense.

385. *bot triste*, i.e. 'without trust'. See Introd. pp. xiv–xv.

391. The meaning is : 'Further, we ought to know of all the days we have dread [of]', the one preposition *of* doing double duty. B reads *Of al þᵉ days we haue to drede ȝitt aw vs to knaw*, and this is clearer. Possibly the scribe began the sentence with the idea of comparing *ane* of l. 392 with all the other days to be dreaded, viz. 'Of all the days . . . one', and broke off in his construction in the second half of l. 391.

394. *þᵉ hey iustys*, 'the Chief Justice', i.e. Christ. For *high* in the sense of 'chief', cp. 'high road', 'high altar', etc. The Last Judgement is described in the terms of a court of law, which forensic conception was very general in medieval times. Cp. *Cursor Mundi* (ed. Morris, vol. iii, p. 1299), 'þe domes mon [i.e. Christ] shal come to deme'; *The Golden Legend* (Temple Cl. iv. 251) where the devil claims a man's soul, 'for I have thereof an instrument public'; *Prayer to Bl. V.* (*Wheatley* MS., ed. Day, p. 14) where the author begs Mary to save him at the Last Day,

'For als iustice of lyuerance we þe calle,
Þat God hath sett to help vs all.
Þi commission is trewe and large,
Þerfore to me be schelde and targe,
And thole neuer dome passe me agayn,
Bot saue me euer fro endles payn.'

sysse, i.e. 'assize'. The word with *great* or *last* prefixed is often used in ME. literature to refer to the Last Judgement; cp. *The Pricke of Consc.*, l. 5514: 'at þat grete assys'.

398–9. The meaning is : 'There no gold nor fee [nor] relations may be our surety'.

maynpryce, i.e. the legal term for (1) the action of making oneself legally responsible for the fulfilment of a contract or undertaking by another person, suretyship; (2) the action of procuring the release of a prisoner by becoming surety for his appearance in court at a specified time. It is here used figuratively in the sense of 'bail'.

402. *alane*, i.e. 'only'; this is the B reading, which has been adopted as it makes better sense than *onane*, i.e. 'anon', of A, which is only a metrical tag.

404. *count*, i.e. 'account, reckoning', the Last Judgement being regarded as a reckoning or account of our stewardship. The B reading *courte* continues the picture of the court of law.

405. The meaning is : 'All, both bondsmen and freemen, shall there be plaintiffs'. This conception of Death the Leveller, with a definite bias against those who have been mighty, rich or fair in this world was general

Notes

in the Middle Ages. Cp. stanzas xxviii, xxxv–xxxvii of this poem, and see also the poems in Morris's *Old English Miscellany* which refer to this subject, viz. *On Serving Christ, A Luve Ron, Long Life, Doomsday, Death.*

409. *a grete lorde es he.* This sentence is used parenthetically.

413. *and*, adopted from B. The A reading *in* makes no sense.

414. *role of recorde*, i.e. the roll containing the official report, or the material points, of a cause at law. The phrase continues the conception of the Last Judgement as a trial at law, the 'roll' being the legal equivalent of 'the books' in Revelation xx. 12.

417. *seke*, i.e. 'go'. The word is widely used in this sense in ME. It means 'go in quest of', in l. 152, and 'go to visit or help', in l. 435.

419. *is*, adopted from B text to improve the sense of the line. This necessitates, for metrical reasons, the omission of the second *with* before *fyre* in A.

with water and fyre. The doctrine that the world shall end by fire is Biblical, and in addition *Cursor Mundi* (ed. Morris, vol. iii, p. 1290, etc.) quotes Moses as authority for saying that, on the eighth day before the end, the sea will rise over dale and hill and drown all things, that it will rise up to heaven, and the fish will flee to earth. On the tenth day, we are further told, all the saints and heaven will be afraid, the angels will quake, and St. Peter will be dumb for fear (cp. ll. 423–9 of this poem). On the fifteenth day the earth will burn away, and it is the end of all things. Then a trumpet will blow and the Judge will come. In the Old English poem, *Be Domes Dæge* (ed. Lumby, p. 9), there is another reference to the end of the world; the earth will shake, we are told, there will be the fearful noise of the boisterous sea, and fire will consume all.

420. *flye*, i.e. 'flee'. See *O.E.D.* for the confusion of forms of *fly* and *flee*.

422. *he*, so in B whereas A gives *we*, which makes little sense. This line is loosely connected with the preceding one in giving the reason for Christ's anger.

423. *þofe scho wold gyff hyre*, i.e. 'though she would give payment', *hyre* < OE. *hȳr* meaning ' reward, payment, wages '. The idea may be that Mary would be willing to repay her faithful servitors by pleading for them at the Last Judgement, but, as the sentence stands, it seems to mean that Mary would be willing to bribe the Judge to have mercy on sinners. B rather weakly reads: *yf scho walde desyre.*

430. This stanza gives a loose rendering of Matt. xxv. 42–5.

þᵉ werkes of mercy . . . seueⱳ, i.e. the Seven Corporal Works of Mercy, as distinguished from the Seven Spiritual Works of Mercy. These works were so classified in the Middle Ages. Matt. xxv. 35, 36, and Tob. xii. 12 are the basis for the Seven Corporal Works of Mercy, which constantly appear in medieval art, e.g. Van der Weyden's triptych in Madrid

Museum, and the illuminated *Biblia Sacra* (Br. Mus. Add. MS. 17,738 f. 3 v.).

434. *eueñ*, adopted from B. A reads *neuer* here and at the end of l. 436, so that both these lines in A fail to rhyme with ll. 430 and 432.

436. *þat wolde I here neueñ*, i.e. ' I should like to hear (you) say that.' The A reading, *þat wolde ȝe here neuer*, does not rhyme.

437. *by-stedde*, i.e. 'beset', the preterite tense. M E. *bistad*, from *bi-, be-* + *stad*, later *sted*, ' placed,' <ON. *staddr*, pp. of *steðja*, 'to stop, place', was used only as a passive past participle, according to *O.E.D.* which also gives *bestad(de)* as an earlier form of *bested* and used only in the passive voice, but by Spenser made a past tense and active participle meaning ' beset ', viz. *F.Q.* III. v. 22, ' But both attonce on both sides him bestad', and *Sh. Cal.*, Aug. 7, ' What the foule euill hath thee so bestadde '. Here we have the verb used as a past tense long before Spenser. Folio 101 of MS. A is damaged at the edge, so that the endings of some words at the ends of lines are missing. These have been supplied with the help of B and enclosed in square brackets. See ll. 431, 433, 437.

446. *bus*, i.e. '(it) behoves'; the contracted form of the 3rd sing. of the verb *behove* is chiefly used impersonally in ME.

449. *thies Iustyce*, i.e. ' these judges, magistrates '. The plural use of the word *justice* in this sense is, as *O.E.D.* tells us, difficult in early quotations to separate from the word in the sense of ' persons administering the law, a judicial assembly or court of law'. Cp. *Cursor Mundi*, vol. ii, ll. 14854-5 : 'If ani man war tan for oght He suld be-for iustijs (*v. rr.* Iustice, Iustis) be broght '.

mellarse, i.e. 'discoursers, disputers'. This word is neither in *O.E.D.* nor in *E.D.D.*, but it is probably the plural noun < the ME. verb *mellen, medlen, maþelen,* <*OE. maþelian, mæþlan,* 'to speak, discourse ' . Cp. ME. and OE. *maþelere,* 'a discourser.' The phrase would therefore mean: 'These justices and discoursers (or disputers) of law and of learning '. The B reading is *domes men*, i.e. ' judges, deemsters '.

453. The meaning is : ' Just as they erstwhile gave judgement ', *are* being the adverb meaning ' before '. For the general idea of the whole stanza cp. the ME. poem, *On Serving Christ* (*OE. Misc.* Morris, p. 91) :

  ' Nis so wlonk vnder crist ridynde on stede,
  Ne þeos crefty clerekes þat vpe bok rede,
  For gold ne for seoluer ne for glysyinde wede,
  For al þe weole and þe wyn þat riche men fede,
  For seolk ne for cendal ne for deore [wedes],
  Þat ne schal at þe dom beon demed of heore dedes. '

454. *myghtis*, i.e. ' power '; see note to l. 239.

456. *Thire ladyse*, i.e. ' these ladies '; *thire* is the Scotch and Northern form of the demonstrative adjective, cp. *þer* in l. 341. The clothing and adornment of women was the subject of much criticism on the part of

Notes 33

medieval writers and preachers. The extravagant dress of women caused Noah's Flood, we are told in *The Book of the Knight of La Tour-Landry* which, in chaps. xlvii-xlix, liii, denounces the lofty head-dresses and the furred garments then in vogue, as well as the practices of painting, dyeing the hair and plucking the brows. See also *Cursor Mundi*, vol. iii, p. 1550.

457. *revers*, 'revers', i.e. parts of a coat, vest, bodice, etc. turned back so as to exhibit the under-surface ; or the word can mean the material with which the reversed edges are covered. The earliest use of the word given in *O.E.D.* is 1869.

gyde, i.e. a kind of dress or gown. The word is from OF. *guite*, meaning some article of clothing, according to Godefroy, a hat. In the fifteenth century we find both ME. forms, *gyte* (*gite*) and *gide* (*gyde*, *guyde*). Cp. Chaucer, *Reeve's T.* 34, 'She cam after in a gyte of reed', and *Chester Pl.* (Shak. Soc.) ii. 187 :

> ' Fie on pearles ! fie on pride !
> Fye on gowne ! fye on guyde.'

Peele in the late sixteenth century uses the word to mean 'splendour, brightness, magnificence ', e.g. ' dim is David's glory and his gite'. (*David and Beth*. VII. 82, *Works*, ed. Bullen, II.)

458. *bendys*, i.e. 'bands, fillets, or straps, used for ornament or as part of a dress'. Cp. *Cursor Mundi*, vol. iii, l. 28016: 'With bendes broud and colers wide'.

botonys, i.e. 'buttons', often used for ornamentation ; cp. *Gaw. and Gr. Knt.* 220 : ' On botounz of þe bryȝt grene brayden ful ryche'. B reads *meroures*, 'mirrors'.

felettis, 'fillets', i.e. ribbons or narrow bands of material used for binding the hair, or bound round the head to keep the head-dress in position or merely for ornament.

fare, i.e. 'apparel', a derivative meaning of ME. *fare* <OE. *faru*, 'a going, a journeying ', hence 'equipment for a journey, apparel'.

459. *garlandis*, i.e. 'chaplets' of costly material, especially of gold or silver work ; cp. Chaucer, *Rom. of Rose*, 869:

> ' Of orfrays fresh was hir gerland ;
> I, whiche seen have a thousand,
> Saugh neuer, y-wis, no gerlond yit
> So wel [y]-wrought of silk as it.'

perry, i.e. 'jewellery'; from OF. *pierrie*.

pryde, i.e. 'magnificent or ostentatious adornment'. The B reading for this line is : ' Golde on þer garlandes perly and pride'.

460. *kelles*, i.e. 'hair-nets, caps, or head-dresses'; the Northern form of ME. *calle*, 'caul'. Cp. *Pist. of Sus.*, l. 158 : 'Heo hedde cast of hir calle and hire keuercheue (MS. I kell, courcheffe)'.

corchyfes, i.e. 'head-dresses'. Cp. *Cursor Mundi*, vol. iii, l. 28018 :

D

'Wit curchefs crisp and bendes bright', and *Gaw. and Gr. Knt.*, l. 954, 'Kerchofes of þat on wyth mony cler perleȝ'.

461. This line I take to mean: 'So well-made and gleaming to display next their skin'. The B reading is: 'So schaply *and* semand*e* to schew by þer syd*e*', with *semande*, the Northern form of the participial adjective, *seeming*, meaning 'suitable, fitting'.

462. *myrthe*. This word may mean any of the following: 'joy, cause of joy, entertainment, gratification, gaiety'.

469-70. *be, by*, i.e. 'against'; the preposition is in each case used with pejorative force. The author says that he not only speaks against lords and ladies, but finds much to say against others, viz. the pretenders to gentility. B reads *anely* instead of *alle*, with better effect.

471. The meaning is: 'These gay fellows who make a show of gentility'; *galiarde* can also mean 'valiant, stout, sturdy', and in this sense is applied to Sir Gawain in *Morte Arthure*.

gedlynges, i.e. 'base-born fellows'. The word *gad(e)lyng, gedlyng* is in late MSS. corruptly written *godlinge, geldinge*; see B.

472. *denyvs*, i.e. 'disdainful'; *denyvs* almost certainly = *deignous*, and possibly is a scribal error for *deynus* or *deynous*, a form of ME. *deignous*, which is apparently a shortened form of *dedeignous* < OF. *desdeignous*. The B form *dengyouse* may be an attempt to represent *n* mouillé; cp. *deyneȝouse (Cant. T.* A 3941, Pt. MS.).

473. *purfelle*, i.e. 'embroidered border of a garment'; from OF. *porfil, pourfil*. Cp. *Knight of la Tour-L.*, ch. xxi, p. 30, 'this astate that ye use of gret purfiles and slitte cotes'; and *Pearl*, 216: 'Of precios perle in porfyl pyȝte'. The borders could also be adorned with fur; see *Knight of la Tour-L.*, ch. xxi, p. 30, 'y woŧ furre her gowne, coleres, sleues, and cotes, the here outwarde; thus she shaŧ be beter purfiled and furred thanne other ladies and gentiŧ women'.

peloure, i.e. 'furs or fur trimmings'; from AF. *pellure*, in OF. *peleure, pelure*. Cp. *Rel. Ant.* vol. ii, p. 19: 'hir wede, Purfiled with pellour doun to the teon'. See also *Knight of la Tour-L.*, ch. xxi, p. 31: 'thei furre her colers, that hangin doune into the middil of the backe, and thei furre her heles'.

hedys, i.e. 'the hair dressed in some particular manner', hence 'a head-dress'. For the former sense see *Fabyan Chron.* VII. ccxxiv. p. 251: 'For that tyme clerkes vsed busshed and brayded hedys'. Most probably the reference here is to the monstrous head-dresses of the period, often made of rich material and bejewelled. See *Knight of la Tour-L.*, chs. xlvii-xlix, pp. 62-4, on the subject, e.g. 'she was atyred with high long pynnes lyke a iebet, ... and saide she bare a galous on her hede' (p. 64).

474. *hir*. The poet changes from the generic to the particular, viz. the woman decked out in expensive clothes but ashamed of her humble origin.

479. *schames nane*, i.e. 'no one is ashamed', literally: '(it) shames

Notes   35

none', this being the transitive impersonal use. In l. 480 we have the personal reflexive use.

485. I take this line to mean that we shall all have to appear in person, and no proxy will be allowed, at the Last Judgement. The word *knaue* is caught in the binding of the MS., so that *-e* is missing.

486. The meaning is: ' He judges according to reason or justice, as scholars declare '. The word *thies* which appears in A before *clerkes* is omitted from the text, as it is not in B and the omission improves the sense.

487-9. These lines are based on Matt. xxv. 33. The A reading of the first half of l. 489, ' þair sange es of sorowe *and* swa' departs from the Biblical account and spoils the picture, so B reading has been substituted in the text.

499-500. In this poem, Mary is not so much the queen, sure of her request being granted and saving her clients in spite of her Son's anger (as she is represented so often in medieval literature), but rather the gentle feminine advocate, influential indeed, but finally appalled into silence before the Judge's wrath. See note to ll. 342-7.

502. *folowe þer-to*, i.e. ' strive after it, aim at it ', *folowe* being used figuratively.

506. *whethir-so*, i.e. ' whithersoever ', *whether, whethir* being obsolete forms of the adverb *whither*, the addition of *so* emphasizing the idea of indefiniteness.

we, the reading of B. The *to* of A is evidently a mistake, the word being very possibly repeated from the line above.

508. *techis*, the gnomic present; the lesson continues though the episode is over.

517. *lay*, i.e. ' song '. B reads *walay*, ' lamentation '; see *waly* in *E.D.D.*

520. *salt*, i.e. ' do perforce '; see note to l. 1.

GLOSSARY

It is intended that this Glossary besides giving the meanings of unusual words should also provide an analysis of the language of the poem. It will therefore be found to contain some words of which the meanings are obvious but which have been included for linguistic reasons. Where a word of clear meaning occurs in but one form or with unimportant differences it is given only once, but variants of linguistic significance are noted in full. When a variant form occurs commonly, *etc.* is written after the first line reference.

The few additions needed to make the Glossary serve the purpose of an Index have been made.

a, *a.* a, 1, etc.; one, 317 (*see* Note). *See also* Ane.
A, *interj.* Ah! 27.
Adam, *n.* Adam, 92.
after, *prep.* according to, 91, 484; after, 381.
all, alle, al, *pron., a. and av.* all, 19.
allaṅ, [al]ane, *a.* alone, only, 196, 402. *See* Note.
allanly, *av.* solitarily, by herself, 209.
als, *conj. and av.* as, 3, etc.; as, *conj.* 153, 294, 331.
alswa, *av.* also, 470; also, 178.
amange, *prep.* among, 8.
and, *conj. conditional*, if, 366. *See* Note.
ane, *pron. and a.* one, 392; a, 317 (*see* Note); one, 56; alone, 85. *See* Note *and see also* A.
appered, *v. pt. 3 s.* appeared, 294.
appill(e), *n.* apple, 95, 98; nappill, 104. *See* Note.
appoṅ, appon, *prep.* upon, 149, etc.; apon, 394; vp-on, 311.
appostills, *n. pl.* Apostles, 294.
arayede, *v. pt. p.* arrayed, 456.
ar(e), *v. See* Be.
are, *conj. and av.* ere, 374, 453 (*see* Note); or, *conj.* 294, 337, 357.
as, *conj. See* Als.
aske, *v. imper. 1 pl.* ask, 335; *pt. 1 s.* askede, 432.
assaye, *v. inf.* try with afflictions, test, 340. *See* Note.
asse, *n.* ass, 148.
at, *prep.* (*introd. infin. of purpose*) to, 340, 408, 460.
attir, *n.* gall, 203.
atyre, *n.* attire, 417.
auṅgelle, *n.* angel, 107.
away, a-way(e), *av.* away, 254, 462.
awe, *v. impers.* (it) behoves, is the duty of, 73, 391. *See* Note.
awen(ṅ), *a.* own, 91.

ay, aye, *av.* ever, 63; for ay, 490.
aysell, *n.* vinegar, 203.
badde, *a.* bad, 250.
bale, *n.* torment, grief, woe, 119; *pl.* balls, 46, 246; bales, 389.
bandis, *n. pl.* hinges of a gate, *esp.* the long strips of iron extending across the surface by which it is hung on the crooks, 259.
bane, *n. coll. s.* bony structure of the body, 198; bone, 509.
baptiste, *v. pt. 3 s.* baptized, 173. *See* Note.
barne, *n.* child, 149.
barounes, *n. pl.* barons, 446.
barres, *n. pl.* stakes or rods of iron or wood used to fasten a gate, 260.
bathe, *a.* both, 316; bothe, 405.
be, *prep.* by, 42, 213; bi, 79 (*see* Note), 225; by, 229, 277; be, by, against, 469, 470. *See* Note.
be, *v.* be; *inf.* 55, etc.; bee, 39, 97; *subj. pr. 1 s.* be, 20; *subj. pr. 2 s.* be, 60; *subj. pr. 3 s.* be, 127, 250, 339; *subj. pr. 1 pl.* be, 337, 366, 466; *pt. p.* bene, 123, 262, 406; *pres. 2 s.* arte, 117; art, 251; *pres. 3 s.* es, 28, etc.; is, 63, 72; *pr. 1 pl.* are, 363, 364, 380; *pr. 3 pl.* are, 82, etc.; ar, 331; er, 43; *pt. 1 s.* was, 7, etc.; *pt. 3 s.* was, 138, etc.; *pt. 1 pl.* were, 403, 410; *pt. 3 pl.* were, 271; ware, 454; *subj. pt. 3 s.* were, 120, 285, 387; ware, 239; *subj. pt. 1 pl.* were, 345.
beaute, *n.* beauty, 25.
be-come, *v. pt. 3 s.* became, 129.
bedde, *n.* bed, 435.
bedde, *v. pt. 3 pl.* offered, 203; *pr. p.* bedande, reciting in prayer, saying, 4. *See* Note.
Bedleṁ, *n.* Bethlehem, 147.
be-fore, *prep. See* Bifore.
begyṅ, be-gyṅ, by-gyṅ, *v. inf.* begin,

Glossary

41, 387, 478; *subj. pr. 3 s.* bygyn̄, 65; *pt. 3 s.* by-gane, bigan̄, 88, 105; *pt. 3 pl.* bi-gane, bigane, 5, 187.
be-halde, *v. intr. imper. 2 s.* look, 122. *See* Note.
b[elde], *v.* abide, dwell; *inf.* 316 (*see* Note); belde to, raise or construct gradually, 6 (*see* Note); *pt. 3 s.* beldede, dwelt, 147.
belle, *n.* bell, 33. *See* Note.
belyue, *av.* quickly, eagerly, 96.
bemys, *n. pl.* trumpets, 393.
bendys, *n. pl.* straps, bands used for ornament or as part of dress, 458. *See* Note.
bere, *n.* bier, 358.
bere, *v. inf.* bear, 511, 110 (*see* Note); *pres. 3 pl.* 353; *pt. p.* borne, 201; *inf.* bere, bear (a child), 120; *pt. p.* borne, 110, 149, 158.
berying, *verb. n.* burial, 437.
besoughte, *v. pt. 1 s.* besought, 37.
bete, *v.* relieve; *inf.* 46; *pt. p.* bett, 119.
be-tyme, *av.* in good time, early, 465.
betyn̄, *v. pt. p.* beaten, 198.
bewes, *n. pl.* branches of trees, 5; bowes, 6.
bi, bi-. *See* Be, Be-.
bifore, bi-fore, by-fore, *prep.* before (place), 190, 309, 343, 375, 445; be-fore, 415; bi-forne, 108 (*see* Note); bi-fore (time), 512.
bi-gyled, by-gylede, *v. pt. p.* deluded, cheated, disappointed, 320, 345.
bi-houes, *v. impers. pres.* (it) behoves, 404.
bileue, *v. pres. 1 s.* believe, 94.
birde, *n.* maiden, girl, 25.
birde, *n.* bird, 46; *pl.* birdis, 5.
bla, *a.* livid, lead-coloured, bleak, 212.
blawe, *v. inf.* blow, 393.
ble, *n.* colour, complexion, 212; blee, 46, 180.
blenke, *v.* blanch, pale; *inf.* 180; *pt. 3 s.* blenkede, 212.
blissede, blyssede, *v. pt. p.* blessed, 39, 127, 313, 339; *pt. 3 s.* blyssed(e), 33, 297, 509; *ppl. a.* blyssede, 149.
blode, *n.* blood, 202, etc.; blude, 245.
blomes, *n. pl.* blooms, 2.
blossomes, *n. pl.* blossoms, 2.
blude, *n. See* Blode.
blyn̄, *v.* cease, desist, stop; *inf.* 389; *subj. pr. 1 pl.* 465.
blythe, *a.* joyous, glad, 110.
bodworde, *n.* message, announcement, behest, 110, 250.
body, *n.* body, 33; *pl.* bodyes, 406.
boghte, *v.* redeemed; *pt. 3 s.* 327; *pt. p.* 245, 333.
[bolde], *a.* bold, 188.
bon̄, *a.* good, 268.
bondage, *n.* bondage, 327; bonddage, obligation, 332. *See* Note.
bone, *n. See* Bane.
borowe, *v. inf.* save, ransom, 468.
bot, *conj.* but, 96, etc.; except, 95, 260, 402, 504; ne non . . . bot, 355; bot, unless, 336; bot if, unless, 56, 65, 463; bot, *prep.* without, 385 (*see* Note); *av.* only, 255.
bote, *n.* relief, rescue, helper, 139.
bothe, *a. See* Bathe.
botonys, *n. pl.* buttons, 458.
bour[es], *n. pl.* glades, arbours, 6. *See* Note.
bowes, *n. See* Bewes.
braste, *v. pt. 3 pl.* broke suddenly under violent pressure, 260.
brathely, *av.* violently, furiously, 201.
breke, *v. inf.* break, 259.
brighte, *a.* bright, 2, 46. *See also* Bryghte.
broghte, *v.* brought; *pt. 3 s.* 156, 262; *pt. 2 pl.* 437; *pt. p.* 246, 268, 271, 358.
bryghte,*n.* beautiful woman, a 'fair', 147. *See* Note.
buke, *n.* book, 33. *See* Note.
burgeon̄, *v. inf.* bud, sprout, 6.
burghe, *n.* town, 147.
bus(e), *v. impers.* (it) behoves, is obligatory upon, 379, 446. *See* Note.
by, *av.* by, 219.
by, by-. *See* Be, Be-, Bi-.
byde, *v. inf.* await, 385; remain, continue to be, 227; *pr. 1 pl.* bide, 332.
bygg, *a.* big, 201.
bysohopis, *n. pl.* bishops, 446.
by-stedd[e], *v. pt. 3 s.* beset, hard pressed, 437. (*Not in O.E.D. as preterite.*) *See* Note.
by-twix(e), *prep.* between, 148, 278.

calle, *v. inf.* call, 107; *pr. 1 pl.* 382; *pt. p.* callede, 404.
care, *n.* care, 22; *pl.* cares, 349.
carpe, *v.* talk; *pres. 3 pl.* 475; *ppl. a.* carp[and], chattering, prating, 292 (*see* Note); *verb. n.* carpyng, speech, 28.
casten̄, *v. pt. p.* cast, 221; *verb. n.* castyng, losing, 59.
catele, *n.* property, wealth, goods, 474.
changynge, *verb. n.* changing, 59.
ohaste, *a.* chaste, 137. *See* Note.

Glossary 39

chere, *n.* cheerfulness, 32; countenance, aspect, 211.
childe, *n.* child, 158; *pl.* childe[r], childre, childir, 160, 166, 268.
chosen̄, *v. pt. p.* chosen, 137.
cite, *n.* city, 160.
clathe, *n.* cloth, 361.
cled[de], *v. pt. p.* clothed, 433.
clere, *a.* bright, beautiful, fresh, 58, 84 (*see* Note), 118, 354; innocent, 176.
clerke, *n.* scholar, cleric, 368; *pl.* clerkes, 294, 486.
closede, *v. pt. p.* enclosed, confined, 234, 337.
coloure, *n.* colour, complexion, ruddy colouring, 59, 84 (*see* Note), 354; *pl.* colours, colours, 2.
Coloyne, *n.* Cologne, 151.
comandis, *v. pr. 3 s.* commands, 328.
come, *v.* come; *inf.* 30; *pr. 3 s.* commes, 250, 355; *pr. 3 pl.* comme, 382; *pt. 3 s.* come, 108.
comforthe, *n.* comfort, 28.
comforthe, *v.* assist, relieve, encourage, comfort; *inf.* 32, 227; *pr. 3 pl.* comforthes, 86; *pt. 3 s.* comforthede, 220; *pt. 2 pl.* 436.
comly, *a.* comely, beautiful, 84, 118; *n.* fair one, 32.
conceite, *n.* secret, confidential knowledge, 56.
consayue, *v. inf.* conceive, 118; *pt. p.* consayuede, 122.
conynge, *verb. n.* learning, erudition, knowledge, 368.
corchyfes, *n. pl.* kerchiefs, 460 (*see* Note); kertchefs, 16.
corse, *n.* body, dead or alive, 365, 474.
cosyn̄, *n.* cousin, 122.
couer, *v. inf.* restore, 32.
couere, *v. inf.* cover, 460.
count, *n.* account, answering for conduct, 404. *See* Note.
Criste, Cryst, *n.* Christ, 289, 293, 409, 421.
crosse, *n.* cross, 199; crose, 280.
croun̄, crown̄, *n.* crown, 311, 353.
crownned, *v. pt. p.* crowned, 199.
crysome, *n.* chrisom-cloth or robe, 402.
crystened, *v. pt. p.* christened, 403.
curtase, *a.* gracious, 84. *See* Note.

damysels, *n. pl.* damsels, young unmarried ladies, 472.
Dauyd, *n.* David, 263.
dede, *a.* dead, 20, 235, 239; *n.* 396.
dede, *n.* death, 166, 279, 355, 437.

dede, *n.* doing, performance, action generally, 484.
degree, *n.* estate, condition, 93, 440.
dele, *v. pr. 3 pl.* have intercourse or dealings, 472.
deme, *v.* judge, condemn, sentence; *inf.* 184, 189; *pt. 3 pl.* demyd, 453 (*see* Note); *pt. p.* demede, 484.
denyvs, *a.* disdainful, haughty, 472. *See* Note.
dere, *a.* dear, 170; noble, 352.
derlynge, *n.* best beloved, favourite, 263. *See* Note.
deuocyoun̄, *n.* devotion, 310.
dewe, *a.* true, genuine, proper, 352. *See* Note.
dide, *v. pt. 3 s.* caused, 11, 228.
diffadynge, *verb. n.* fading, losing freshness or fairness, 58.
discypilis, *n. pl.* disciples, 301.
dole, *n.* grief, mourning, 162.
dolven̄, *v. pt. p.* buried, 235.
dome, *n.* judgement, trial, sentence, 192, 452, 482; *pl.* domes, 455.
domesdaye, *n.* Day of Judgement, 497.
doun̄, down̄, *av.* down, 309, 355.
dowte, *n.* doubt, 71.
drawes, *v. pres. 3 s.* draws, 355. *See* Droughe.
drede, *n.* dread, 386, 391, 499; cause of dread, danger, 191.
drede, *v. inf.* dread, 482.
dredfull, *a.* awe-inspiring, 424, 500; dredefull, terrible, 355.
drery, *a.* cruel, dire, 192; sad, 211.
droughe, *v.* drew; *pt. 1 s.* 12; *pres. 3 s.* drawes, 355.
duelle, *v. inf.* delay, tarry, 31 (*see* Note), 163; dwell, 366, 372; *pres. 1 pl.* duell, 507.
dy(e), *v.* die; *inf.* 189, 218; *pt. 3 s.* dyede, 514.

eghne, *n. pl.* eyes, 344; *s.* ey, 299.
Egippe, *n.* Egypt, 164.
[e]lde, *n.* old age, 123. *See* Note.
Elezebeth, *n.* Elizabeth, 123.
ellis, *av.* otherwise, 345.
emelle, *av.* in the midst, 263.
emperour, *n.* emperor, 190; *pl.* emperours, 447.
ensample, *n.* example, 172.
er, *v. See* Be.
erelles, *n. pl.* nobles, 447.
es, *v. See* Be.
Eue, *n.* Eve, 92.
[euen̄], *av.* even, 434; euyn̄, directly, straight, 308.

Glossary

euer-mare, euer-more, *av.* evermore, 507, 57.
euerylke, *a.* every, 381. *See* Note.
ey, *n.* eye, 299; *pl.* eghne, 344.

face, *n.* outward form, semblance, 91; ? person, 114. *See* Notes.
fadir, *n.* God the Father, father, 135, 476; *gen. s.* 130, 315.
faile, *v.* fail; *pr. subj. 3 pl.* 27; *pr. 3 s.* failes, 359; *pt. 3 s.* faylede, 304.
falle, *v.* fall; *inf.* 140, 208; *pr. 1 pl.* die, 357 (*see* Note); *pt. 3 pl.* felle, fell, 102; *impers. pres.* falles, (it) is allotted, 369. *See* Note.
falowe, *v.* fade, wither, pale; *inf.* 208; *pt. 3 s.* falowede, 237, 274.
famen, *n. pl.* foemen, foes, 175.
fande, *v. See* Fynde.
fare, *v.* go, travel; *inf.* 241, 369, 445; *pr. 1 pl.* 374; *pr. 3 s.* fares, 52.
fare, *n.* commotion, display, apparel, 251, 458 (*see* Notes); multitude, troop, 383.
fay, *n.* faith, allegiance, 304.
fayne, *a.* glad, well-pleased, 99, 285; *av.* gladly, willingly, 175, 476.
[fela], *n.* associate, companion, peer, 144; felawe, 80; *pl.* felawes, 76.
felauchip, felawchipe, *n.* companion, company, companionship, 197 (*see* Note), 359.
felde, *n.* field, country as opposed to town or village, 359.
felde, *v. pt. p.* brought low, 383.
fele, *pron.* many, much, 45, 470; *av.* fele-folde, many times over, 155.
fele, *a.* fell, cruel, 175. *See* Note *and see also* Felle.
fele, *v. pr. 1 pl.* feel, 357.
felettis, *n. pl.* fillets, 458. *See* Note.
felle, *a.* dire, painful, 267, 369; fele, fell, cruel, 175. *See* Notes.
felle, *n.* skin, 281, 410.
fende, *n.* fiend, devil, 99.
fer[cost], *n.* a kind of boat or ship, 331. *See* Note.
fere, *n.* comrade, companion, partner, 34, 80, 174, 408.
ferly, *n.* wonder, 285.
ferre, *av.* far, 44, 369.
ferthe, *pron. and a.* fourth 137, etc.; f[ourte], *a.* 144.
feste, *v. pt. p.* fastened, 51.
fete, *n. pl.* feet, 200.
fett, *v. inf.* fetch, 408.
feyntely, *av.* feebly, 51.
fle, *v. inf.* flee, 496.

flesche, *n.* flesh, 281, 410.
fl[ode], *n.* flood, waters, 331.
flom, *n.* river, 173.
floures, *n. pl.* flowers, 8.
flye, *v. inf.* flee, 420. *See* Note.
folowe, *v. inf.* strive, aim, 502. *See* Note.
folys, *n. pl.* sins, 496.
fonne, *pron.* few, 360.
forbede, *v. pt. 3 s.* forbade, 94.
for-gaffe, *v. pt. 3 s.* forgave, 266.
for-getyn, *v. pt. p.* forgotten, 364.
foule, foulle, *n.* bird, 27, 40.
fra, *prep.* from, 229, 279, 411, 468; froo, 102. *See* Note.
frayne, *v. inf.* ask, 251.
frayste, *v. pt. p.* asked, tried, 383. *See* Note.
fre(e), *a.* free, noble, gratuitous, abundant, 24, 35, 326, 502; *n.* free, freemen, 405.
frendys, frendis, *n. pl.* friends, 103, 170.
frere, *n.* friar, 356.
froo, *prep. See* Fra.
ful, full, *a. and av.* full, 40, 308.
fune, *v. pt. p.* found, 466. *See* Fynde.
fynde, *v.* find; *inf.* 50, 290; *pr. 1 s.* 470; *pr. 1 pl.* 76, 375; *pr. 2 s.* fyndis, 66; *pt. 1 s.* fande, 44; *pt. p.* funden, 45; fune, 466.
fyre, *n.* fire, 419.

ga, *v.* go; *inf.* 280, 506; goo, 103, 109 (*see* Note); gane, 146, 171, 200; *pt. p.* gane, 400.
Gabriel, Gabryel, *n.* Angel Gabriel, 107, 114, 132.
gadir, *v. inf.* gather, assemble, 409.
gaffe, *v. See* Gyff.
galiarde, *a.* lively, gay, spruce, 471. *See* Note.
[g]alle, *n.* gall, 204. *See* Note.
gamen, *n.* mirth, delight, 307.
gan, gane, *v. pt. 3 s.* did, 161, 214; gon, gonn, 146, 251, 265, 280; gun, 107; *pt. 3 pl.* gan, gane, 166, 200, 241, 258, 259.
gane, *v. See* Ga *and* Gan.
gare, *v. pr. 1 pl.* cause, 350; *pt. 3 s.* garte, 159. *See* Note.
garlandis, *n. pl.* chaplets, coronets, 459. *See* Note.
garte, *v. See* Gare.
gaste, *n.* spirit, 273 (*see* Note); Holy Ghost, 81, 135, 316.
gate, *n.* way, 378.
gedlynges, *n. pl.* low-born fellows, 471. *See* Note.

Glossary 41

gentil, *a.* gentle, noble, 314; *av.* gentill, excellently, nobly, 142.
gentry, *n.* rank, style and dress of gentlefolk, 471. *See* Note.
gestis, *n. pl.* guests, temporary inmates, 252.
giffes, *v. See* Gyff.
glade, *v. inf.* make glad, 252.
gladenesse, *n.* joy, alacrity (in action), 86.
glasyng, *verb. n.* gliding, slipping, 379. *See* Note.
glew[e], *n.* joy, 307.
glyde, *v. inf.* glide, go, 379, 463.
gode, *n.* God, 317, 514; *gen. s.* goddis, 79; God, 128.
godhede, *n.* Godhead, 241, 279.
gon(ñ), *v. See* Gañ.
goo, *v. See* Ga.
gownne, *n.* gown, 457.
graoious, graoyouse, *a.* gracious, 342, 515.
grauntede, *v. pt. 3 s.* granted, 514.
graythede, *v. pt. p.* prepared, made ready, 378.
grene, *a.* green, 95, 104.
grete, *a.* great, 162, etc.; gret, 205, 393, 394; grett, 378.
grett, *v. pt. 3 s.* greeted, saluted, 113, 132.
greued, *v. pt. p.* aggrieved, 421.
grew, *v. pt. 3 s.* grew, 319.
gryse, *v. inf.* tremble with terror, be greatly afraid, 392.
grysse, *n.* individual plant of grass, 66.
gude, *a.* good, 286; *n.* 329.
gud fryday, *n.* Good Friday, 514.
gudnesse, *n.* goodness, 86.
guñ, *v. See* Gañ.
gyde, *n.* a kind of dress or gown, 457. *See* Note.
gyff, *v.* give; *inf.* 423; *pr. 3 s.* giffes, 328; *pt. 3 s.* gaffe, 192.

habyde, *v. intr. inf.* wait, remain, 446; *trans. pt. 3 pl.* habade, awaited, 242.
hade, *v. See* Haue.
hafe, *v. See* Haue.
halde, *v. imper. 2 pl.* hold, 75.
hale, *a.* healed, sound, 289, 303. *See* Note.
hally, *av.* entirely, completely, 72, 125, 333.
halowe, *a.* holy, 306 (*see* Note); *n. pl.* halowes, saints, 426.
haly, *a.* holy, 135, 171, 240, 261, 273, 316; holy, 81.
hande, *n.* hand, 70; *pl.* handis, 200.

hande-maydeñ, *n.* handmaid, 124.
hande-werke, handwerk(e), *n.* a thing wrought by hand, 106, 171, 240, 261.
harde, *v. See* Here.
hardely, *av.* with hardihood or courage, hare, *n.* hair, 460. [62.
hase, *v. See* Haue.
hastily, *av.* quickly, 150.
hasty, *a.* quick, 370.
hate, hatte, *a.* hot, 228, 380.
haulle, *n.* hall, 111.
haue, *v.* have; *inf.* 169, 489; hafe, 314, 330, 501; *pres. 1 s.* hafe, 21, 42, 44, 45; *pres. 3 s.* hase, 38, etc.; *pres. 1 pl.* hafe, 341, 383, 392, 391; haue, 497; *pr. 2 pl.* haue, 431, 433; *pr. 3 pl.* hase, 144, 294; *pt. 3 s.* hade, 106, 244; *pt. 3 pl.* hade, 262; hadde, 455; *subj. pt. 2 s.* hade, 56.
haylsede, *v. pt. 3 s.* saluted, 115.
he, *pron.* he, 31, etc.; hee, 424; *acc.* hym, 73; *dat.* hym, 153; *gen. See* Hys. *See also* pay.
hede, *n.* head, 16, 311; *pl.* hedys, coiffures, head-dresses, 473. *See* Note.
heghe, *a.* high, 111. *See also* Hey.
hele, *v. inf.* conceal, keep secret, 476.
helle, *n.* hell, 171, 241, 261, 370.
hende, *a.* gracious, kind, 316, 321. *See* Note.
Herawde, *n.* Herod, 157.
herde, *v. See* Here.
here, *v.* hear; *inf.* 28, 53, 404, 436 (*see* Note); *pt.* herde; *1 s.* 517; *3 s.* 157; *3 pl.* 257; *pt. 2 pl.* harde, 432.
heried, *v. pt. 3 s.* harried, despoiled, 261. *See* Note.
herkeñ, *v. inf.* harken, 28.
hert, *n.* heart, 125; *gen. s.* 289, 333. *See* Note.
heueñ, *n.* heaven, 70. *See* Note.
hewe, *n.* colour, form, complexion, 59, 303.
hey, *a.* chief, 394 (*see* Note); heghe, high, 111; hye, 473; *av. phrase* appoñ hey, on high, 183.
hir, *pron. and a. See* Soho.
his, *pron. and a. See* Hys.
holy, *a. See* Haly.
hope, *v. pres. 1 s.* anticipate, suspect, 250. *See* Note.
horberd, *v. pt. 2 pl.* harboured, sheltered, 434.
hourres, *n. pl.* prayers or offices appointed to be said at the seven canonical hours, 4. *See* Note.
howseles, *a.* homeless, 434.

hy, *n.* haste, 295.
hyde, *n.* skin, 303, 461.
hye, *a. See* **Hey.**
hym-selfe, *pron.* he himself, 169, 176; *emph.* **hymselfe,** 188.
hyre, *n.* payment, 423. *See* Note.
hys, *poss. a.* his, 408; **his,** 33, etc.; *poss. pron.* **his,** 72, 262.

I, *pron.* I, 3; *acc.* **me,** 12; *dat.* **me,** 20; *gen. See* **My**; *pl.* **we,** 68; *acc.* **vs,** 86; *dat.* **vs,** 73; *gen.* **our(e),** 37.
ilk(e), *a.* same, 79, 80, 131, 322, 415, 510, 515.
ilk, ilk (a), *a.* every, 484, 408. *See* Note to l. 381.
*in-***tiƚƚ,** *prep.* into, 306.
is, *v. See* **Be.**
it, *pron.* it, 51. *See also* **pay.**
iustys, Iustyce, *n. See* **Justice.**
[**i-wys**], **iwysse,** *av.* certainly, indeed, assuredly, 19, 264.

Jewes, *n. pl.* Jews, 187.
Jhesu, *n.* Jesus, 184, 187.
Joħ**n,** *n.* John the Baptist, 173; John the Apostle, 219, 225, 226.
Jordane, *n.* Jordan, 173.
Josephe, *n.* St. Joseph, 146, 163.
joyne, *v. pres. 3 pl.* combine, unite, 142.
Judas, *n.* Judas, 184.
justice, iustys, *n.* judge, 183, 394; *pl.* **Iustyce,** judges, magistrates, 449. *See* Note.

kane, *v.* can; *pr. 1 s.* 193; *pr. 3 s.* **ka**ñ, 368.
kayser, *n.* emperor, 353; *pl.* **kaysers,** 445.
kaytefde, *ppl. a.* imprisoned, 365.
kele, *v. inf. intr.* become cool, 78; *trans.* assuage, 349.
keƚƚe, *n.* a woman's hair-net, cap, or head-dress, 16; *pl.* **kelles,** 460. *See* Note.
kertchefs, *n. See* **Corchyfes.**
[**knaw**], **knaue,** *a.* male, 158, 160; *n.* **knau[e],** male servant, 485. *See* Note.
knawe, *v. inf.* know, 391; be known, 412.
knele, *v.* kneel; *inf.* 350; *pr. 3 s.* **kneles,** 343; *pt. 3 s.* **knelde,** 108; **knelyd,** 309.
knytt, *v. pt. p.* bound, tied, 361.
kyñ, *n. collect.* kinsfolk, 399 (*see* Note), 467, 475, 479.
kynde, *n.* nature, family, kind, 77 (*see* Note), 292.

kynredyñ, *n. collect.* kindred, relations, 382.
kythe, *n. collect.* neighbours, friends, acquaintance, 467.
kythes, *v. pr. 3 pl.* display, 471. *See* Note.

lady, *n.* lady, 34; *pl.* **ladyse,** 456; **ladys,** 469; **our(e) lady,** the Virgin Mary, 37.
lande, *n.* land, 138, 451.
lange, *av.* long, 21.
langede, *v. impers. pret.* (it) longed, yearned, 247.
lare, *n.* learning, 367, 449.
lastis, *v. pr. 3 s.* lasts, 63.
late, *v. imperat. 2 s.* let, 253.
lay, *n.* religious law, 172.
lay, *n.* song, lyric, 517.
layne, *v. inf.* conceal, 253; be concealed, 270. *See* Notes.
leche, *n.* healer, spiritual physician, 286.
lede, *v. subj. pr. 2 pl.* lead, 195.
lefe, *n.* leaf, 68; *pl.* [**lefes**], 67; **leues,** 82, etc.
lere, *v. inf.* teach, learn, 60, 172.
leste, *n.* least, 441.
lett, *n.* hindrance, 136.
lett, *v.* omit, forbear; *inf.* 397; *pt. p.* prevented, 123.
leue, *a.* dear, 185.
leue, *v.* believe; *inf.* 73, 293, 356 (*see* Note); *pr. 3 s.* **leues,** 320; *pt. 3 pl.* **leuede,** 298.
leue, *v.* leave; *imper. 2 s.* cease, 224; *pret. 3 s.* **leued,** left, 202; *pt. p.* **leuede, lefte,** 275, 196.
lighte, *v.* descended (in ref. to the Incarnation); *pt. 3 s.* 128, 132; *pt. p.* [**lyghte**], 145; *pt. 3 s.* **lyghtede,** alighted, 31.
likeñ, *v. See* **Lyke**ñ.
liste, *v. impers. pr.* (it) pleases, 356.
littiƚƚ, *a.* little, 365.
Longeus, *n. See* Longinus, 228. *See* Note.
lorde, *n.* 393, 409; *pl.* **lordis,** 469; **oure lorde,** Christ, 145, 306.
lordynges, *n. pl.* Sirs! Gentlemen!, 185. *See* Note.
lorne, *v. pt. p.* lost, 106.
loue, *v.* love; *inf.* 73; *pt. 3 s.* **louede,** 34, 302.
louely, *a. and av. See* **Lufly.**
lowtte, *v. inf.* bow, make obeisance, 73.
l[u]f, *n.* love, 63 (*see* Note); **lufe,** 40, etc.
lufly, *a.* lovely, 106; **louely,** 144; *av.*

Glossary 43

lufly, beautifully, willingly, 31; louely, 67.
lyken̄, v. liken ; *inf.* 68 ; *pr. 1 s.*
liken̄ bi, represent by, symbolize by, 79. *See* Note.

made, *a.* mad, 254.
made, *v. See* Make.
make, *v.* make ; *inf.* 159, 168, 398 ; *pr. 2 s.* makis, 254 ; *pt. 3 s.* makede, 90 ; made, 7, 92 ; *pt. p.* made, 326.
man̄, *n.* man, 121 ; *pl.* men̄, 472.
manhed(e), *n.* manhood, 239, 242.
many, *a.* many, 43.
mars, *n. a. and av.* more ; *n.* 45, 170, 193, 376 ; *a.* 168, 239, 454, 462 ; *av.* 55 (*see* Note), 493. *See* Euer-mare *and* Neuer-more.
Marie, *n. See* Mary.
Mary, *n.* the Virgin Mary, 18, 226 ; Marie, 109, 115, 124, 499.
maryede, *v. pt. p.* married, 121.
maste, *a.* most, 390, 497 ; *av.* 131.
mater, *n.* matter, 41.
Maudelayne, þe—, *n.* Mary Magdalene, 284, 287.
may, *v.* may ; *pr. 2 s.* 46 ; *pr. 3 s.* 315 ; *pr. 1. pl.* 335 ; *pr. 3 pl.* 168, etc.; maye, 140 ; *pt. 3 s.* myghte, 442 ; *pt. 1 pl.* myght, 330.
May(e), *n.* month of May, 1, 519.
may(e), *n.* maiden, virgin, 7, 238, 508.
mayden̄, *n.* maiden, virgin, 109, 112, 134, 137, 275, 318.
maynpryce, *n.* suretyship, 398. *See* Note.
me, *pron. See* I.
medilerthe, *n.* the earth, 71. *See* Note.
medowes, *n. pl.* meadows, 1, 520.
meke, *a.* meek, 339.
mekill, *a.* great, much, 98 ; *av.* much, 462.
mellarse, *n. pl.* discoursers, disputers, 449. *See* Note.
mercy, *n.* mercy, 266.
mery, merie, *a.* pleasant, delightful, joyous, 4 (*see* Note), 71, 112.
message, *n.* message, 159, 511.
messagere, *n.* messenger, 109. *See* Note.
mett, *v.* met ; *pt. 3 s.* 284 ; *pt. p.* 134; mett with, had carnal knowledge of, 121 (*see* Note) ; arte mett with, hast encountered, 117.
mi, *poss. a. See* My.
mirre, *n.* myrrh, 154.
mode, *n.* heart, courage, spirit, 211, 287, 511, 513.

moder, *n.* mother, 226, 307 ; modir, 223, 275, 423, 476 ; modyr, 318.
morne, *n.* morn, 112.
morne, *v.* mourn ; *inf.* 105 ; *imperat. 2 s.* 224 ; *pr. p.* mournande, 223 ; *ppl. a.* mournande, 211 ; *verb. n.* mournyng(e), 7, 10.
mornynge, *n.* morning, 519; moruenyng, 1.
mot(e), *v. pr. 3 s.* may, 39, 313 ; mott, 97.
moue, *v. inf.* move, 41.
mournyng(e), *verb. n.* mourning, 7, 10. *See also* Morne.
my, *poss. a.* my, 29, 30, 46, 125 ; mi, 30 ; myn̄, 4.
mydwarde, *n.* middle, 474.
myght(e), *n.* might, 129, 276, 318 ; *pl.* myghtis, power, 239, 454. *See* Notes.
mylde, *a.* kind, gracious, merciful, 18.
myn̄, *n.* less, 45.
myrthe, *n.* cause of joy, happiness, rejoicing, melody, 117.
mysdede, *n. collect.* misdoings, 501.
mysse, *n.* wrong-doing, 266.
mysse (off), *v. inf.* fail to obtain, 338.

na, *a.* no, 193, 285, 376, 384, 429 ; no, *a.* 63, 277, 352, 353, 367, 397, etc. ; no, *av.* 493.
nane, *pron.* none, 44, etc. ; non, *a.* 354.
nappill, *n.* apple, 104. *See* Note.
naylede, *v. pt. p.* nailed, 206, 222.
nayles, *n. pl.* nails, 200.
ne, *conj.* nor, 121, etc. ; ne . . . not, *av.* not, 432.
nede, *n.* need, 390, 497.
nere, *av.* near, 30, 55. *See* Note.
neuen̄, *v. inf.* utter, say, 428, 436. *See* Note.
neuer-more, *av.* nevermore, 78.
no, *a. and av. See* Na.
noghte, *av.* not, 31, etc.; [noghte], nogte, *n.* nought, 19, 253. *See* Note *and see also* Not.
non, *a. See* Nane.
not, *av.* not, 469, 485, 488, 502 ; nott, 499. *See also* Noghte and Ne.
no-thynge, *n.* nothing, 85, 94.
notis, *n. pl.* notes, 24.
nyghte, *n.* night, 324 ; [ny3te], 149.

of, *prep.* of, 1, etc. ; off, 87, 338 ; of, off, 16, 232.
offerde, *v. pt. 3 pl.* offered, 153.
on, *prep. See* On(e).

Glossary

onȩ, *pron.* one, 56; *a.* alone, 85. *See* Note *and see also* Ane.
on(ȩ), *prep.* on, in, 3, 5, 306. *See* Note.
or, *conj.* ere, 294, 337, 357. *See also* Are.
orcherde, *n.* garden, 4; *pl.* orcherdis, 43.
oþer, *pron. pl.* others, 470.
our(ȩ), *poss. a.* our, 37.
ourselfe, *pron. emph.* ourselves, 485.
out, owt(ȩ), *av.* out, 111.
oxe, *n.* ox, 148.

pane, *n.* fur, especially as used for lining to garment, 401.
paradise, *n.* heaven, 70 (*see* Note); paradisse, Eden, 93.
paste, *ppl. a.* past, 483.
payn(e), *n.* pain, 255; *pl.* paynes, 377.
peloure, *n.* fur, especially as used for lining or trimming of a garment; furred garments, furs, 473. *See* Note.
pere, *n.* equal, 82.
pereles, *a.* peerless, 116.
perry, *n.* jewellery, 459. *See* Note.
persones, *n. pl.* parsons, 448.
Pilate, *n.* Pontius Pilate, 183.
pitt, *n.* pit of hell, 255 (*see* Note); pytt, grave, 362.
playing, *verb. n.* exercise, diversion, 3. *See* Note.
pouste, *n.* power, 328.
pray, *v.* pray; *inf.* 442; praye, 429; *pr. subj. 3 s.* pray, 336; *pr. subj. 1 pl.* praye, 510.
praye, *n.* prey, the saved, 346.
prelatis, *n. pl.* prelates, 448.
preson, *n.* prison, 436.
preste, *n.* priest, 356; *pl.* prestys, 448.
price, *n.* worth; of price, of great excellence, highly esteemed, 82.
pride, pryde, *n.* pride, pomp, display, splendid adornment, 148, 383, 400, 448, 459 (*see* Note), 481.
purfelle, *n.* embroidered border of garment, 473. *See* Note.
purgatorye, *n.* Purgatory, 371.
putt, *v.* put; *pt. 3 s.* 296; *pt. p.* 380.

quelle, *v. inf.* kill, slay, 161.
qwake, *v.* quake; *inf.* 396; *pr. p.* qwakande, 418.
qwarte, *n.* health, the state of being alive and well, 161. *See* Note.
qwen, *n.* queen, 312.
qwik, *n.* the living, 396.

qwitt, *a.* free, clear, rid (of), 363.

rafe, *v. pt. 3 s.* pulled, tore, 16.
rane, *v. pt. 3 s.* ran, 213, 229.
rasse, *v. pt. 3 s.* rose above horizon, 150. *See* Ryse.
ratheste, *av.* soonest, most of all, 49.
rawe, *n.* row, line; on a —, in a line, 395.
raysede, *v. pt. 3 pl.* raised, 278.
rebanes, *n. pl.* ribbons, 457.
recorde, *n.* official report; role of —, roll containing the official report or material points of a cause, 414. *See* Note.
rede, *a.* red, 213.
rede, *v. pres. 1 s.* advise, command, 194, 510; *imper. 2 s.* reede, 18; *pr. 3 pl.* rede, declare, expound, 486. *See* Note.
reghte, *n.* right; with —, rightfully, properly, 48.
rekenysse, *v. pr. 3 s.* enumerates, mentions in due order, 430; rekkenys, judges, 486. *See* Note.
rekills, *n.* incense, 154.
resoune, *n.* reason, justice; by —, in conformity with reason or justice, 486.
resyñ, *v. pt. p.* risen, 289. *See* Ryse.
retenewe, *n.* train, suite, 265.
revers, *n. pl.* revers, 457. *See* Note.
righte, *a.* fitting, sound, 143; ryght, right, 487; *av.* righte, ryghte, aright, straight, exactly, 18, 190, 453.
robis, *n. pl.* robes, 401; robys, 456.
roche, *n.* rock, 214.
rode, *n.* rood, 235, 269, 327.
role, *n.* roll, 414. *See* Note.
rote, *n.* root, 143.
ryalle, *a.* royal, 450.
ryde, *v. inf.* ride, 450. *See* Ryne.
ryght(e), *a. and av. See* Righte.
ryne, *v. inf.* run, go on one's feet, in opposition to *ride*, 450.
ryse, *v.* rise; *inf.* 395; *pt. 3 s.* rasse, 150; *pt. p.* ryseñ, 283; resyñ, 289. *See also* Vp-rysse.
ryue, *v. inf.* tear or split asunder, 214. *See* Note.

sade, *a.* heavy, 248.
saklesse, *a.* innocent, 186.
sall, *v.* shall; *pres. 1 s.* 60, *pres. 2 s.* 118, 290; salle, 109; *pres. 3 s.* sall, 119, etc.; schall, 443; *pres. 1 pl.* sall, 366, 417, 506; *pres. 3 pl.* sall, 1, (*see* Note), etc.; sal, 396, 489; *pl. 1 s.* solde, 120; *pl. 2 s.* solde, 255;

Glossary 45

pt. 3 s. **scholde,** 158, 180; **sulde,** 208, 216; *pt 3 pl.* **solde,** 103.
samen, *av.* together, 317, 407.
sare, *a.* painful, grievous, 54; *av.* bitterly, grievously, 26.
sary, *a* distressed, sorrowful, wretched, 36, 96, 248.
Sathanasse, Sathanas, *n.* Satan, 96 (*see* Note), 248.
saulde, *v. pt. p.* sold, betrayed, 174, 267; **solde,** 184.
saule, *n.* soul, 241; *pl.* **saules,** 327, 329; **saulles,** 330, 406.
say, *v.* say; *inf.* 193, 300, 186 (*see* Note); *pres. 3 pl.* 438; *pt. 3 s.* **said,** 185, 188; **saide,** 18; **sayde,** 116.
sayn, saynt, *a.* saint, 219, 173.
schaff, *v. See* **Saff.**
schame, *v.* be ashamed; *inf. reflex.* 480; *pres. impers.* **schames,** (it) shames, 479. *See* Note.
schane, *v. str. pt. 3 s.* shone, 150. *See* Note *and see also* **Schynede.**
schaply, *a.* of good or elegant shape, 461. *See* Note.
schawe, *v. inf.* show, 416; **schew,** 443; **schewe,** 397, 461. *See* Note.
schede, *v. pt. 3 s.* shed, 202, 289.
scho, *pron.* she, 10; *acc.* **hir,** 113; *dat.* **hir,** 34; *gen.* **hir,** 11. *See also* **pay.**
scholde, *v. See* **Saff.**
schynede, schane, *v. pt. 3 s.* shone, 150 (*see* Note); *ppl. a.* **schynand,** shining, resplendent, 461. *See* Note.
scorde, *v. pt. p.* kept account of, recorded, 413.
scowrges, *n. pl.* whips, lashes, 198.
seconde, *a.* second, 79, etc.; **secounde,** 131; **secund,** 181.
see, *v.* see; *inf.* 99, etc.; **se,** 231; *pres. 2 s.* **sees,** 255; *pr. 3 s.* **sees,** 492; *pt. 3 s.* **sawe,** 218; *pt. 1 pl.* **sawe,** 439; *pt. 3 pl.* **sawe,** 299.
sekande, *v. pres. p.* sickening, 8. *See* Note.
seke, *v. inf.* seek, 54, 60, 160, 496; *pres. 1 pl.* **seeke,** 381; *inf.* **seke,** go, 417 (*see* Note); *pt. 3 s.* **soughte,** sought, 96; *pt. p.* 21, 42, 44; *pt. 3 pl.* **soughte,** went, 152; *pt. 2 pl.* **soghte,** went to visit or help, 435.
sekenesse, *n.* sickness, 435.
sekir, *a.* sure, certain, reliable, 323, 340, 366, 376.
selcouth, *n.* marvel, 21, 249.
semelye, *n.* assembly, 407.
semly, *a.* fair, handsome, seemly, 83; *n.* **semely,** a 'seemly' person, 108, 186, 300.

sen, *conj.* since, 348.
sende, *v.* send; *inf.* 485; *imperat. 2 s.* 20; *pt. 3 s.* **sent(e),** 34, 111; *pt. p.* **sent(e),** 38, 408.
se[r]e, *a.* separate, 406.
seruyce, *n.* service, 125.
sett, *v.* set; *inf.* 172; *pres. 3 s.* **settis,** 487; *pt. 3 s.* **sett,** 311; *pt. p.* **sett,** 60.
sighe, *v.* sigh; *inf.* 55; *pres. 2 s.* **syghys,** 26; *pt. 3 s.* **syghede,** 237; *pres. p.* **syghande,** 8; *verb. n.* **syghynge,** 54.
sight[e], syghte, *n.* sight, 21, 99, 151, 249, 323.
slyk, *a.* such, 188.
snelle, *av.* quickly, promptly, 159.
so, *av.* 9, etc.; **swa,** 216; **swa,** thus, 276.
socour(e), *n.* succour, 20.
sofferde, *v.* suffered; *pt. p.* 444; *pt. 1 s.* **sufferde,** 267; *pt. 3 s.* 176.
soghte, *v. See* **Seke.**
solde, *v. See* **Saff** *or* **Saulde.**
som, *a.* some, 21; **somme,** 20.
sonderyng, *verb. n.* parting, 411.
son, **sone,** *n.* son, 79.
son, **sone,** *av. See* **Soune.**
sorow(e), *n.* sorrow, 248.
sothe, *n.* truth, 270.
soughte, *v. See* **Seke.**
soune, *n.* sun, 212.
soune, *av.* soon, 20; **son,** 259; **sone,** 364.
sounken, *v. pt. p.* sunk, 331.
soyttures, *n. pl.* petitioners, plaintiffs, 405. *See* Note.
spak(e), *v. See* **Speke.**
speche, *n.* speech, 27.
spede, *v. inf.* succeed, prosper, 488, 495.
speke, *v.* speak; *inf.* 257, etc.; *subj. pr. 3 s.* 512; *pt. 3 s.* **spak,** 222; **spake,** 291.
spelle, *n.* discourse, 27.
spere, *n.* spear, 201; *pl.* **speris,** 162.
spere-schafte, *n.* spear-shaft, 229.
spetide, *v. pt. 3 pl.* fixed or impaled on a sharp weapon, 162.
sprede, *v. pt. p.* stretched, 199.
spryng(e), *v. inf. trans.* bring forth, produce, 1 (*see* Note); *absol.* 520; *intrans. inf.* **sprynge,** grow, 141; *pres. p.* **spryngande,** 57; *pres. 3 pl.* **sprynges,** 305.
stabill, *a.* constant, steadfast, strong, 304, 340.
stalkede, *v. pt. 1 s.* walked softly or stealthily, 14.

Glossary

standis, *v. pres. 3 s.* stands, 225; *pt. 1 s.*
 stode, 14; *pt. 3 s.* 209, 291.
stede, *n.* place, spot, 14, 291.
stedfaste, *a.* steadfast, 340.
steghe, *v. pt. 3 s.* ascended, 306.
steke, *v. inf.* secure, fasten, 258.
sterne, *n.* star, 150.
steueñ, *n.* voice, petition, 427, 432.
stiłł, *a.* unperturbed, silent, 304, 427;
 av. constantly, continually, 126;
 stilly, quietly, 14.
stirre, *v. inf.* set on foot, 98.
stode, *v. See* Standis.
strange, *a.* strong, 377.
strete, *n.* road, 42.
stryfe, stryue, *n.* strife, 277, 98.
sufferde, *v. See* Sofferde.
sulde, *v. See* Sałł.
swa, *av. See* So.
swelte, *v. pres. 1 pl.* faint, are overcome, 357.
swete, *a.* sweet, charming, delightful, 40, 127.
swilk, *a.* such, 138, 319; swylk, 440.
swouñ; *v.* swoon, *pres. 1 pl.* 357; *pt. 3 s.* swounede, 215.
syde, *n.* side, 225; *pt.* sydes, 213.
syghande, *v. See* Sighe.
sympiłł, *a.* simple, 417.
syn, *n.* sin, 176, 480; *pl.* synnes, 397.
synfułł, *a.* sinful, 422.
synge, *v. inf.* sing, 5.
syre, *n.* lord, master, 421.
sysse, *n.* assize, 394. *See* Note.
sythe, *n.* life-time, 55. *See* Note.
sythen, sythyñ, *av.* then, afterwards, 90.
sytt, *v. inf.* sit, 394.

taghte, *v. See* Techis.
take, *v.* take; *inf.* 166, 452; *pres. subj. 2 pl.* 194; *imper. 2 s.* 225, 226; *pt. 3 s.* tuk, 264; toke, 98, 280; *pt. p.* taken, 197, 232; tane, 144, 177.
tale, *n.* account, story, 190.
tane, *v. See* Take.
techis, *v. pres. 3 s.* teaches, 508 (*see* Note); *pt. 3 s.* taghte, taught, 301.
tełłe, *v.* tell; *inf.* 157, 368; *pres. 1 s.* tełł, 469; *pt. 3 s.* tolde, 288; *pt. p.* to[lde], 190; *inf.* telle, count, 265.
temple, *n.* temple, 214.
tene, *n.* malice, 100.
þair(e), *poss. a.* their, 253, etc.; þer, 320; theire, 166.
þam, *pron. See* þay.
than, þan, þañ, thane, *av.* then, 23.
thankkede, *v. pt. 3 s.* repaid, 155.
þare, thare, *av.* there, 65, 192, 452,
 492; þer, 149, 263, 398, 405, 420, 422, 488; þer-in, therein, 372; þer-to, after it, at it, 502 (*see* Note); *obj. gen.* þerof, þer-of, thereof, 151, 368.
thare, *v. impers. pres.* (it) is necessary, 253. *See* Note.
þase, *dem. a.* those, 8, etc.
þat, *rel. pron.* who, which, that, whom, 7, 21, 56, etc.; what, 244, 374.
þat, *demons. pron. and a.* that, 14, etc.; *pl.* þase, 8, etc.
þat, *conj.* that, 120, etc.; when þat, when, 431, 502; were þat, where, 366.
þay, *pron.* they, 141, etc.; *acc.* þam̃, 93, etc.; *dat.* þam̃), þam, 94, 98, etc.; *gen. See* þair(e).
þe, the, *a.* the, 5, 6, etc.; *av.* 168, 239.
thedyr, *av.* thither, 417.
theire, *poss. a. See* þair(e).
þer, *a. and av. See* þair(e), þare *and* Thire.
þer, *rel. av.* where, 43, 291, 324 (*see* Note), 472.
ther, þer, þare, there, *unemph. av.* there, 63, 97 (*see* Note), 148, 150, 277, 379, 467, 504.
thi, þi, *poss. a.* thy, 25, 27, etc.
thies, *demons. a.* these, 140, 144, 288, 449, 471; þis, these, 157. *See* Note.
thirde, *pron. and a.* third, 81, 242, 277.
thire, *demons. a.* these, 456; þer, 341. *See* Notes.
þis, this, *demons. a. and pron.* this, 19, etc. *See also* Thies.
þof, *conj.* though, 239, 353; þofe, 423.
thoghte, *n.* intention, imagination, trouble, 15, 29.
Thomas, Tomas, *n.* Thomas the Apostle, 288, 290, 291. *See* Note.
Thoresday, *n.* Thursday, 306. *See* Note.
thor[ne], *n.* thorn-branches collectively, 199.
þou, thou, *pron.* thou, 18, etc.; *acc.* þe, the, 60, 439; *dat.* þe, the, 29, 253 (*see* Note); *gen.* (*see* Thi); *pl.* 3e, 186, etc.; *dat.* 3ow, 193; *gen.* (*see* 3our).
thre, *a.* three, 136; three, *a. and pron.* 164, 181.
thritty, *a.* thirty, 174.
thrugh, *prep.* through, 279; thurgh, 4, etc.
þus, thus, *av.* thus, 111.
tiłł, *prep.* to, 201, 424, 500; *conj.* till, 76, 246.
to, *av.* too, 382.
to, *prep.* to, 5, etc.; at, 122; as, for, 225.
to-gedir, *av.* together, 81.

Glossary

to-ȝere, *av.* this year, 122.
toke, *v. See* Take.
townñ, *n.* town, 359.
tray, *n.* deceit, trick, 64.
trayste, *v. inf.* trust, 133.
tree, *n.* tree, 12, etc.; cross, 206; tre, cross, 222, 232; plant, 319. *See* Note.
tremland, *v. pr. p.* trembling, 418.
tresoñ, *n.* breach of faith, 64, 133.
treuthe, trewthe, *n.* truth, 185, 301.
trewe, *a.* true, faithful, loyal, reliable, 54, 133, 238, 301, 508.
trewe-lufe, trew-lufe, trewluf, trewlufe, *n.* quatrefoil, true-love, 42 (*see* Note), etc.; *gen. s.* trewlufe, 167; trewlufe grysse, true-love grass, quatrefoil, 66.
triste, *n.* trust, 385. *See* Note.
trone, *n.* throne, 83.
trow, *v. imper.* 2 *s.* believe, 290.
trye, *v. inf.* demonstrate, prove, 185.
tuk, *v. See* Take.
turtitt, turtytt, *n.* turtle-dove, 23 (*see* Note), 508.
twa, *a. absol.* two, 214, 278, 504.
twyñ, *v. inf.* separate, part, 216.
tyde, *n.* time, hour, 223, 297.
tyme, *n.* time, 387, 483, 495.
tythynges, *n. pl.* tidings, news, 157, 288.
tytte, *av.* quickly, at once, 177.

vmbsett, *v. pt. p.* encompassed, beset, 419.
vmthynke, *v. reflex. pres.* 1 *pl.* call to mind, bethink, 392.
vndir, *prep.* under, 12.
vn-fayne, *a.* ill-pleased, sorry, 249.
vnglade, *a.* unhappy, sorry, 463.
vnsely, *a.* wicked, unhappy, 157.
vn-titt, *prep.* unto, 223. *See also* Vn-to.
vn-to, *prep.* unto, to, 80, etc.
vp-on, *prep.* upon, 311. *See also* Appoñ.
vp-rysse, *v. inf.* rise from the dead, 396.
vs, *pron. See* I.

vesett, *v. pt.* 2 *pl.* visited, 435.

waa, *n.* woe, distress, affliction, 97, 274; wa, 210, 372, 489, 505; wo, 30.
wafutt, *a.* full of woe, afflicted with misfortune, 488.
wakkeñ, *v. inf.* stir up, call into existence, 97.
walde, *v. See* Witt.
wandrethe, *n.* misery, distress, 30.

wanne, *a.* gloomy, dark, 89.
ware, *v. See* Be.
warre, *a.* aware, 7.
was, *v. See* Be.
wate, *v. See* Wete.
way(e), *n.* way, road, path, 42; *pl.* wayes, 369, 370.
we, *pron. See* I.
wedde, *ppl. a.* wedded, 163.
weddede, *v. pt.* 3 *s.* married, 146.
welde, *v. pres.* 1 *s.* possess, hold, enjoy, 19; *pres.* 3 *s.* weldis, 69; *pt.* 3 *s.* weldide, handled with skill, plied, 264.
wele, *n.* wealth, happiness, 19, 348, 505.
wele, *a.* happy, fortunate, 322; *av.* well, 74.
welle, *n.* spring, source, 3 (*see* Note), 348.
welthe, *n.* wealth, 72, 236, 462.
wende, *v. imper.* 2 *s.* depart, 254; *pt.* 1 *s.* went(e), went, 3, 518; *pt.* 3 *s.* wente, 300.
wene, *v. pres.* 1 *s.* think, expect, 49.
wepe, *v.* weep; *inf.* 351, 491; *pt.* 3 *s.* 210; *pres.* 3 *s.* wepys, 344; *verb. n.* wepynge, 11, 224, 346.
were, *v. See* Be.
were, *dep. interr. av.* where, 366.
werkes, *n. pl.* works, 341.
werlde, *n.* world, 19.
weryede, *v. pt. p.* cursed, 97.
wete, *v. inf.* know, 13; wiete, 15; wytt, 372; *pres.* 1 *pl.* wate, 384.
wexe, *v. pt.* 3 *s.* became, 212, 249.
weyssely, *av.* wisely, cleverly, 47.
whañ, *rel. pron.* whom, 73.
whare, *rel. av. and conj.* where, 57, 66.
wha-so, *pron.* whoever, 320; who-so, 371, 495.
what, *rel. and interr. pron.* what, 186, 255; who, 251.
whethir-so, *av.* whithersoever, 506. *See* Note.
whi, *interr. av.* why, 26, 350.
whitts, *conj.* while, 335.
who-so, *pron. See* Wha-so.
wiete, *v. See* Wete.
wighte, *n.* creature, 127, 352; wyghte, 322, 367; *pl.* wyghtis, 488.
wilde, *a.* unruly, unreasonable, 15, 341.
witt, *n.* will, 13.
witt, *v.* will; *pres.* 1 *s.* 110; *pres.* 2 *s.* 189; *pres.* 3 *s.* 349, etc.; *pres.* 3 *pl.* 502; *pt.* 1 *s.* walde, 13, 15, 29, 41; wolde, 436; *pt.* 3 *s.* walde, 31, 163, 169, 170, 293; wold, 423; wolde,

476; *pt. 1 pl.* wolde, 330; *pt. 2 pl.* wold[e], 186; *pt. 3 pl.* walde, 175; wolde, 153; *subj. pt. 2 s.* wald, 47; walde, 30.
wit͡h, *prep.* with, 22, etc.
wit͡h-in, *av.* within, 69.
wit͡h-owte, *av.* without, 69.
wit͡howtten, with-owtten, *prep.* without, 58.
witte, *n.* wit, 53.
wo, *a.* grieved, sorrowful, 182; woo, 101.
wold(e), *v. See* Wilt.
wonder, *a.* wondrous, 53.
wondis, *n. pl.* wounds, 229, 267, 281, 298, 443.
[w]one, *v. pres. 3 pl.* dwell, continue to be, 81.
woo, *a. See* Wo.
worde, *n.* word, 428; *pl.* wordis, 188.
woughe, *n.* injury, harm, 11.
wrange, *v. pt. 3 s.* wrung, 17, 210.
wreche, *n.* wretch, 422.
wrenke, *n.* trick, artifice, 420.
wrethede, *v. pt. p.* made angry, 341.
wretyn, *v. pt. p.* written, 413.
wroghte, *v. trans. pt. 3 s.* made, 70; *pt. p.* 244; *intr. pt. 3 s.* wrog[hte], behaved, moved restlessly or convulsively, 17.

wrothely, *av.* sorrowfully, bitterly, 17.
wry, *v. inf.* turn, go, 475.
wyde, *a.* wide, 229.
wyfe, *n.* wife, 275; wyffe, 163.
wyghte, *n. See* Wighte.
wyle, *n.* wile, 420.
wyn͡, *v.* win; *inf.* 47, 388; *pres. 3 s.* wȳnnes, 346; *subj. pr. 1 pl.* wyn, 463; *inf.* wyn͡ vn-to, make or find one's way to, 513.
wynde, *n.* wind, 89.
wyse, *a.* wise, 367.
wysse, *v. inf.* show the way, 47, 420.
wytt, *v. See* Wete.
wytter, *a.* evident, 444.

ȝare, *a.* ready, prepared, 503.
ȝare, *av.* quickly, soon, immediately, certainly, well, 61, 194 (*see* Note), 217, 235, 243, 375, 456.
ȝatis, *n. pl.* gates, 258.
ȝe, *pron. See* þou.
ȝitt, *av.* yet, 44, 170; ȝit, 391; still, 60. *See* Notes to ll. 60 and 391.
[Ynde], *n.* India, 288. *See* Note.
ynoughe, *a.* enough, 10.
ȝode, *v. pt. 3 s.* went, 215.
ȝole, *a.* Christmas, 149.
ȝo*ur*, ȝoure, *poss. a.* your, 75, 227, 267.

The manufacturer's authorised representative in the EU for product safety is Oxford University Press España S.A. of El Parque Empresarial San Fernando de Henares, Avenida de Castilla, 2 - 28830 Madrid (www.oup.es/en or product.safety@oup.com). OUP España S.A. also acts as importer into Spain of products made by the manufacturer.
Printed and bound by CPI Group (UK) Ltd, Croydon, CR0 4YY

20/03/2026

02075339-0004